I am delighted to see this classic st
by Prof. Renwick come back int
a theological student in the 196

since that time. It is written with the two qualities Calvin desired
for his own literary productions: clairty and brevity. It holds one's
attention from beginning to end. I have lived in and out of Scotland
for the last 40 years, and it has been my impression that in general,
Scotland has become ashamed of its Reformation, at least since
the 1970s. These days people tend to think of Mary Queen of
Scots as the heroine, and John Knox as a vicious partisan, if not
a villain of the time. For these reasons, we need to read chapter
1. The Pre-Reformation Church; chapter 10. The Principles of
the Scottish Reformation; chapter 12. The Queen Returns, and
especially, chapter 14. Was John Knox Right? Prof. Renwick was
certainly pro-Reformation, but his historical scholarship is well-
grounded and fair, and he refrains from any censoriousness in
these controversial issues. Greatly recommended!

Douglas F. Kelly
Professor of Systematic Theology,
Reformed Theological Seminary,
Charlotte, North Carolina

Arguably the Reformation had more impact on the Scottish
nation than on any other. The story of how the preaching of
God's Word changed a whole society, with an impact which ripples
down still today, is a thrilling and moving one. A.M Renwick's
small book on the Scottish Reformation is the best introduction
to the period. I am delighted that on the 450th anniversary of
the Scottish Reformation this superb book is being reissued.

David Robertson
Minister,
St Peters Free Church,
Dundee, Scotland

First published half a century ago, the reappearance of this gripping account of the Scottish Reformation is greatly to be applauded. Its depth of research, extent of coverage and clarity of presentation, all combine to make Renwick's study one of the finest and most eminently readable introductions available on this most exciting period in Scotland's history.

Tom Lennie
Author,
Glory in the Glen: A History of Evangelical Revivals in Scotland 1880–1940

Increasingly our people are interested in their roots, whether geneaological or spiritual. Here in this little book A. M. Renwick provides us with a way to trace where we've come in such a way to help us know where the church needs to go. Get out your shovel and dig into the history of the Scottish Reformation!

Sean Michael Lucas
Senior Minister,
First Presbyterian Church,
Hattiesburg, Mississippi

THE STORY
OF THE
SCOTTISH REFORMATION

A.M. Renwick

CHRISTIAN
HERITAGE

Dr A.M. Renwick was professor of Church History at the Free Church College in Edinburgh.

Copyright © Christian Focus Publications 2010

ISBN 978-1-84550-598-1
10 9 8 7 6 5 4 3 2 1

First published in 1960
Reprinted in 2010
by
Christian Focus Publications Ltd,
Geanies House, Fearn, Ross-shire,
IV20 1TW, Scotland, Great Britain
www.christianfocus.com

Cover design by Moose77.com

Printed by
Bell and Bain, Glasgow

Mixed Sources
Product group from well-managed
forests and other controlled sources
www.fsc.org Cert no. TT-COC-002769
© 1996 Forest Stewardship Council

FSC

CONTENTS

PROLOGUE

The Reformation was not only a spiritual force, but also a far-reaching social and political element in the history of the world. Although it came to Scotland somewhat later than to Germany, Switzerland and England, in no other country was it so thorough. It reached to the very heart of the nation, and affected every aspect of life. All Europe realized the tremendous need for reform in the Church, but not all nations became Protestant, and of those which did, not one established such a radical reformation as did the little kingdom of Scotland. Some countries, for example Germany, although they did a mighty work in establishing Reformation and have made all of us their debtors, nevertheless stopped short of carrying the Reformed doctrines to their logical conclusion. It was not so in Scotland for, from the beginning, the aim of the Reformation leaders was to set up an ecclesiastical polity founded on the New Testament. In support of their tenets, and of the Presbyterian system which they adopted, they appealed directly to apostolic teaching.

During long years the people had struggled for liberty. To them independence was something of priceless value. Racially,

The legacy of Scottish reform

they were a mixture descended from brave and individualistic Celts; from Norsemen who had the fearless blood of the sea rovers in their veins; from Saxons, many of whose ancestors came to Scotland because they hated Norman feudalism. This freedom-loving people reacted strongly when they realized the spiritual bondage in which they had been held by the Roman hierarchy. Indeed this love of liberty had often manifested itself before the Reformation, even in ecclesiastical affairs, as in the famous Declaration of Arbroath sent to the pope in 1320.

This spirit has frequently been characteristic of mountain people, and it is no accident that the religious history of Switzerland and that of Scotland developed along similar lines. In both countries the Reformed leaders were distinguished by courage, foresight, and ability; this was particularly true, indeed, of John Knox who breathed the spirit of both countries after his long residence on the continent. Like the French, the Scots were blessed with a strong logical faculty and they were not afraid to follow their principles to their proper issue. The French Reformed Church, following with consistency the teachings of its illustrious fellow-countryman, John Calvin, was developing along lines almost identical with the Scottish Church, and was progressing in an astonishing manner, when the diabolical Massacre of St Bartholomew's Eve in 1572 almost suffocated it in blood. From that wicked blow the French Protestant Church never fully recovered.

The Celtic Church

In explaining the phenomenal success of the Reformation in Scotland, we must not overlook the old Celtic Church. Too often we forget what a debt we owe to the men of this Church who, after the barbarians had overrun the Roman Empire, maintained in the West the old culture and the older type

The Legacy of the Celtic Church.

of Christianity in a purer form than on the continent where both had been much adulterated by the pagan influences brought in by the barbarians. This Church was a Bible-loving Church, as is shown by the amazing devotion with which the Holy Scriptures were copied. It was a Church which gloried in preaching at a time when the Roman Church was forgetting the art and devoting itself to endless ecclesiastical rites, especially the Mass. It was also an evangelical Church, proclaiming salvation to sinners through the merits of 'Jesus Christ, and him crucified'. Furthermore, it was a Church tenacious of its independence, and so for centuries it fought strenuously against absorption by the Church of Rome. The Culdees, who inherited the spirit of this Church, maintained their testimony in some places in Scotland till the end of the thirteenth century. Indeed, even today there are many districts in Scotland where the Celtic Church still exercises a subconscious influence upon the people. There can be no doubt that at the Reformation its tradition made it easier for the Scots to revolt against Rome.

The corruption of the Roman Church in Scotland, although it was no worse than in other countries at that time, aroused the ire of both nobles and people, as is clearly seen in the literature of the period. When the most learned theological disquisitions would not have moved the commonalty, they were deeply stirred by the rapacious and sensuous lives of the prelates and priests. The Church was in sad decay and ready to fall, and when the new teaching came through Patrick Hamilton, George Wishart, and the later Reformers, as well as through a flood of literature, the people were in the mood to hear. It was certainly not a case of one man imposing his will upon the nation, as is so often stated.

From the first, the Scottish Reformers took the Bible as, unquestionably, the supreme standard. No other people have

9

ever done so more wholeheartedly. In the Scriptures they saw God's message. They learned the tremendous truth of His sovereignty. The Lord was reigning. He was 'king above the floods'. His will would prevail in spite of all His enemies could do. Hence the calmness with which the Scottish Reformers confronted the mighty of the earth, knowing that they were but men.

When Knox became leader of the Reformation in his country, he was radical in applying the democratic political principles he had embraced. In this respect, he was far ahead of Luther and Calvin, and his strong, virile people were quick to respond to this lead. His teaching did more than that of any other to make the Scots a democratic nation with a democratic Church. Men were shown that they could make a direct approach to God through the mediation of Christ without the intervention of priest or prelate, and in the ecclesiastical courts the clergyman and the layman had exactly the same power.

It is important to bear in mind that Scotland was pivotal in the great political struggle which was going on in Europe at the time of the Reformation. The great aim of France, Spain, and the Emperor, was to crush England, a Protestant country then rising into prominence. For their designs, it was of paramount importance to secure Scotland as a base of their operations. This was why they championed so strongly the claim of Mary of Scotland (then wife of the Dauphin) to be also Queen of England. Most Roman Catholics held that as Henry VIII had divorced Catherine of Aragon in spite of the pope's opposition, his marriage to Anne Boleyn was invalid, and Elizabeth was illegitimate. Many Roman Catholic Englishmen were ready to fight, with continental support, to place Mary of Scotland, a staunch Catholic, on the throne, as the next heir. Hence the vast importance of the reconciliation between England and Scotland at the Reformation. It enabled them both to maintain their independence, and to continue upholding the Protestant faith. *Not keen on this political slant as allowing the Reformation to work.*

The fourth centenary of the Reformation in Scotland was celebrated in 1960, and this brief work aims at recalling some of the stirring events of that great turning-point in the history of the country. *Note the following points: What the book will examine*

1. An attempt is made to picture the position of the Roman Church in Scotland during the half century preceding the Reformation. From the facts presented, it is obvious that serious spiritual decadence had set in, a decadence which was all the more grave because it was at its worst among the prelates. It is clear that nothing but a root and branch Reformation of the Church could save the situation.

2. It has been necessary to give a good deal of attention to the political movements of the time for these had a very direct bearing upon ecclesiastical affairs and sometimes imperilled the rising Reformed Church.

3. The different ways in which the new religious ideas found entry into Scotland are noted, and the manner in which these ideas laid hold of the hearts of confessors and martyrs, whose zeal and example brought almost the whole land under the sway of the Protestant doctrine, is described.

4. The behaviour of independent and restless nobles, who sometimes had scant respect for the central government, is taken into account, especially during the long minorities of James V and his daughter, Mary Queen of Scots. As many of the nobles and gentlemen were protagonists of the Reformed faith, their actions were of special importance. No sketch of the Scottish Reformation could fail to

consider the place of Mary of Lorraine, the Queen Mother, who was regent immediately before the Reformation, and of her daughter, Queen Mary, who ruled in the succeeding years. As both were fervent Roman Catholics, in close league with the pope and the Catholic rulers of Europe, their character and doings assume much importance in the narrative, for they strained every nerve to keep Scotland in the Catholic fold and in alliance with France.

5. Much space is naturally given to John Knox who undoubtedly was the hero of the Scottish Reformation. It will be seen that his dominating personality, his eloquence, his shrewd judgement, his pithy language, and his strong appeal to the masses, contributed more than any other human influence in bringing about the speedy victory of the Reformation.

6. Notice is taken of the special features of the Reformation movement in Scotland where it differed from that in other lands, but it is never forgotten that in those days the Spirit of God was stirring mightily the hearts of men in Germany, Switzerland, England and other countries. In the last resort, the Reformation in Scotland, as elsewhere, was a work of God. Great as were the leaders who fought the battle for truth and righteousness, they would have failed were it not that the Spirit of God worked through them.

In the following pages we shall see how the truths of the gospel laid hold of the souls of many, transforming their lives and making them heroic in the service of God until, finally, their labours were crowned in the complete triumph of the Reformation.

1

THE PRE-REFORMATION CHURCH

There are some who regard the pre-Reformation Church as 'an amiable and lovely maiden' with no spot on her beautiful vesture. They stand entranced as they contemplate the gorgeous services, the stately cathedrals, the altars solemnly railed off from the ordinary worshippers, the Mass, the incense, the well-ordered processions, and the sensuous music. They are greatly impressed by the high potentates of the Church, especially the pope. It all seems so awe-inspiring and so grand. The admirers of such an order of things do not wait to enquire how such elements entered the Church of Christ, or what authority there is for them. Did the apostles approve such forms of service and the characteristic doctrines of the Roman Church? Why are these services so gorgeous and sensuous while the apostolic Church, and the early Church generally, rejoiced in forms of service which were the very essence of simplicity? The Christian Church at the beginning deliberately chose these simple forms, not because the Church must be spiritual, and spirituality does not consist in piling up awe-inspiring rites and ceremonies, or in the multiplying of costly and splendid vestments. All these were well known in ancient times. The service in the Jewish temple was itself ornate, yet the apostles, led by the Holy Spirit, put that aside as having served its purpose in the Old Testament economy. They stressed the religion of the heart rather than outward trappings. If it is ritual for which we are looking we have a long way to go before we can equal the splendour and magnificence of the ancient pagan religions.

When the Church abandoned the ancient simplicity and introduced the endless paraphernalia which characterized medieval ecclesiasticism, did it lead to greater spirituality in the Church? Did men become more Christ-like? Did the high functionaries of the Church develop a character more like that of the apostles when they began claiming so loudly to be *apostolic*? Did the grave departures from the doctrines and practices of the primitive Church produce the fruits of righteousness or did not the Church rather fall into iniquitous practices utterly unworthy of the Christian faith?

For generations before the Reformation, loud cries had been going up from Church Councils and other ecclesiastical gatherings demanding reform of the flagrant abuses which were bringing same upon the Christian cause. The tragedy of the situation, however, was that the members of the Church Councils themselves were the worst offenders. In spite of all that art and wealth could do, the moral condition of the Church remained deplorable in the extreme. Although 'long drawn aisles and fretted vaults' were beautiful to look upon, and 'pealing anthems' swelled 'the note of praise', and grandeur of all kinds surrounded religious rites, yet the Church's spiritual life was feeble in the extreme. Never were beauty and art so much used in the service of the Church; seldom has the moral life of its members been so low.

The situation in Scotland was similar to that in the rest of Europe. The scathing words of John Colet, Dean of St Paul's, to the prelates and priests in his famous sermon to Convocation in 1512 could be applied equally well to Scotland. He declared that reform must begin with the bishops, and that once begun, it would spread to the clergy and thence to the laity; 'for the body follows the soul; and as are the rulers in a State, such will the people be'. He then proceeded to deal in scathing terms with the flagrant abuses which prevailed.[1] To understand the sad conditions of the Church in Scotland, then, we cannot do better than consider the evidence of Roman Catholic writers and the findings of Roman Catholic Councils. They cannot be accused of prejudice against their own faith.

Ignorance and Inefficiency

In 1552 a Catechism was prepared by order of Archbishop John Hamilton with the praiseworthy object of instructing the people in the Ten Commandments, the Creed, the Sacraments, and the Lord's Prayer. It was issued 'with the advice and counsel of the bishops and other prelates' in the Provincial Council at Edinburgh. It was recognized 'that the inferior clergy of this realm, and the prelates, have not, for the most part, attained such proficiency in the knowledge of the Holy Scriptures as to be able, by their own efforts, rightly to instruct the people in the Catholic faith and other things necessary to salvation, or to convert the erring'.[2] It was ordered that the book be regularly read by vicars and curates, 'vested in surplice and stole', on all Sundays and holy days, and the statute then continued: 'The said rectors, vicars, or curates must ... prepare themselves with all zeal and assiduity for the task of reading (in public), by constant, frequent, and daily rehearsal of the lesson to be read,

1. T.M. Lindsay, *The Reformation*, 1, pp. 165 ff.
2. David Patrick, *Statutes of the Scottish Church*, pp. 143, 144.

lest they expose themselves to the ridicule of their hearers, when, through want of preparation, they stammer and stumble in mid-course of reading.[3] This emphatic instruction from the Provincial Council of 1552 shows that many having pastoral charges were bordering on illiteracy. The proceedings of the same Council, seven years later, show that no improvement had taken place. There was ample ground, therefore, for the taunt of the jerring rhymester who wrote:

'The curate his creid he culd nocht reid.'

The Provincial Council of 1549 had declared that many curates were 'very deficient, as well in learning, morals, and discretion.'[4] It is not surprising that at that time the clergy were held in derision. According to George Buchanan many of them were so ignorant of the Scriptures that they believed the *New* Testament was a recent book written by Martin Luther, and declared they would adhere to the *Old* and have nothing to do with the New.[5] When that eminently pious and cultured man, Thomas Forret, Canon of Inchcolm and Vicar of Dollar (often called Dean Thomas), was reprimanded by Bishop Crichton of Dunkeld for preaching 'the Epistle or Gospel every Sunday to his parishioners' because he might make the people think that the bishops should preach likewise, he was advised to preach only when he found 'any good Epistle, or any good Gospel'! When Forret declared that he could find no evil Epistle or evil Gospel, and asked the Bishop to declare which were good and which evil, the latter vehemently replied, 'I thank God that *I never knew what the Old and New Testament was*. Therefore,

---

3.   David Patrick, *Statutes of the Scottish Church*, p. 146

4.   *Op. cit.*, p. 110.

5.   George Buchanan, *History of Scotland*, p. 219.

Dean Thomas, I will know nothing but my portuise and pontifical'.[6] At Forret's trial, the public prosecutor pulled a New Testament out of his sleeve and shouted, 'Behold, he has the book of heresy in his sleeve, which makes all the confusion in the Kirk.' Explanations and expostulations were in vain, and this most attractive character was burnt on the Castlehill of Edinburgh, on 1 March 1539. Four other godly men were burnt in the same place that same day.

Nowhere was the ignorance of the clergy more scathingly denounced than in the *Panegyricus* addressed by Archibald Hay, a cultured priest, to his kinsman, David Beaton, when he became Archbishop of St Andrews and Primate of all Scotland. He wrote: 'I declare, as I desire God's love, that I am ashamed to review the lives of the common and even of certain other priests, obscured all round with the darkness of ignorance, so that I often wonder what the bishops were thinking of when they admitted such men to the handling of the Lord's body, when they hardly knew the order of the alphabet. Priests come to that heavenly table who have not slept off yesterday's debauch ... '[7]

Preaching

For nearly a thousand years preaching had almost vanished from the Church of Rome, its place being taken by the various rites and ceremonies which had been gradually introduced, especially the Mass, in which the priest professed to offer up anew in sacrifice the very body and blood of the Lord Jesus. The altar thus became an object of great veneration, and the man who ministered there and claimed to have the power of

---

6. Thomas McCrie, *Sketches of Scottish Church History*, pp. 16, 17; Calderwood, *History*, I, pp. 126, 127. Portuise = breviary; Pontifical = a book containing the rites.

7. *Ad. D. Davidem Betoun Card. Panegyricus*, fol. XXXIV. Trans. in D. Hay Fleming, *Reformation in Scotland*, p. 42.

turning the bread and wine into the very body and blood of our Lord became of indescribable importance. Through his ministration of sacramental mysteries the grace of God was supposed to come to sinful and needy men, and did not come in any other way. The rites performed by the officiating priest were all that mattered and the proper place of preaching in the Church was lost sight of.

Although the rise in the thirteenth century of the mendicant preaching friars, the Franciscans and Dominicans, made a difference in certain places, yet before the Reformation degeneracy set in even with them, and in Scotland as elsewhere preaching was generally given a very minor place indeed. Again and again Provincial Councils in Scotland had given injunctions to the clergy to preach, but in vain. Not one of the bishops *could* preach in the time immediately before the Reformation, but, in view of the success attending Protestant preaching, the bishops were instructed to emulate them. At Ayr, Gavin Dunbar, Bishop of Glasgow, tried to do so. It proved a fiasco, for he had uttered only a few sentences when he had to apologize to his audience saying, 'They say that we should preach: why not? Better late thrive than never thrive. Have us still for your bishop, and we shall provide better for the next time'.[8] The bishop had desired to counter the preaching of George Wishart in Ayr. Instead, he hastily left the town, and did not attempt to preach there again. The attitude of the pre-Reformation Church in this matter was certainly not that of the Church of the apostles.[9] It ought to be recorded, however, that the good Bishop James Kennedy of St Andrews, who died in 1465, was a notable exception in this respect.

---

8.   John Knox, *History*, 1, p.61.

9.   Cf. 1 Corinthians 1:18, 21.

Irreverence

One might have expected that, in a Church which aimed at making its rites deeply impressive and cultivated magnificent display, one would have found a holy reverence in every place of worship. This was far from being the case. On 1 February 1552 Parliament passed an Act against those who 'made perturbation in the kirk in time of divine service' preventing the Word of God from being heard. They would 'not desist therefore for any monition' of the churchmen. That same year Archbishop Hamilton's Catechism referred to 'the common sin of quarrelling and wanton singing in the kirk on Sunday', and to those who occupied themselves 'in vain, evil, or worldly talking, laughing and scorning'.[10]

This irreverence was well exemplified in connection with the mystery or miracle plays which for generations were a feature of ecclesiastical life. What Sir Walter Scott wrote in a note to *The Abbot* shows the scandalous pass to which the situation had come. He described how the laity (who had been encouraged in their evil course by the clergy) used to elect some 'lord of the revels, who under the name of the Abbot of Unreason, the Boy Bishop, or the President of Fools, occupied the churches, profaned the holy places by a mock imitation of the sacred rites and sang indecent parodies on hymns of the Church'. Sir Walter, who was an authority on medieval institutions, both ecclesiastical and civil, marvelled at the indifference of the clergy to these indecent exhibitions and coarse humour.[11] The profanity became so blasphemous that Parliament had to impose stern penalties.

---

10. T.G. Law's edition of Hamilton's *Catechism*, pp. 68, 69.
11. Sir Walter Scott, *The Abbot*, note E.

Low Clerical Morality

The most distressing feature of all in the pre-Reformation Church was the appallingly low state of morals among the clergy, who were all pledged to lives of celibacy. A witness of unimpeachable authority is Father Archibald Hay (afterwards Principal of St Mary's College, St Andrews) already referred to. In his long *Panegryicus* to Cardinal Beaton he wrote: 'If I proceeded to review the inordinate desire of glory, the incredible cruelty, passion, envy, hate, treachery, the insatiable longing for vengeance, the wicked words and disgraceful actions, all of which rage in the breasts of the churchmen, no one would believed that monsters so savage lurked under a human countenance. I will not treat of the riotous living of those who, professing chastity, have invented new kinds of lusts, which I prefer to be left unknown rather than be told by me.'[12] There is no indication that the cardinal did anything to improve the situation. He could scarcely do so, for in spite of his exalted ecclesiastical position, he was himself a notoriously immoral man. Anyone can verify this by looking up the entries in the Register of the Great Seal of Scotland, 1513 to 1546. There they will find the records of the legitimization of eleven of the Cardinal's bastard sons and three daughters. The father of these is very clearly designated as 'David, Cardinal priest of the Roman Church, Archbishop of St Andrews, Primate of Scotland,' and so on. No one seems to have seen the incongruity of a 'celibate' priest being the father of so numerous a family, as many as twenty according to some authorities. Certain of them married into the highest families in the land, the daughters receiving princely dowries. All this is astonishing when we

---

12. Archibald Hay, *Panegyricus*, fol. XLIII, quoted by D. Hay Fleming, *Reformation in Scotland*, pp. 42-45.

remember that married priests were rigorously condemned, sometimes even to death, as in the case of Norman Gourlay at Edinburgh in 1534.

That the cardinal was not the only offender against sound morals in the Church is proved by the findings of the Provincial Council at Edinburgh in 1549. This gathering of prelates and priests presided over by John Hamilton, who succeeded Beaton as Archbishop of St Andrews and Primate of Scotland, acknowledged that 'the great dissensions and occasions of heresies' were caused principally by 'the corruption of morals and profane lewdness of life in churchmen of almost all ranks, together with the crass ignorance of literature and of all the liberal arts'.[13] Let it be remembered that these are not the words of an over-zealous Protestant, but of a solemn Provincial Council of the Roman Church. This 'Holy Synod and Provincial Council' resolved 'to apply remedies and put a check on these mischiefs, so far as it can adequately to the exigency of the times'. The Council fulminated against the keeping of concubines by churchmen and ordered the prelates and 'their subordinate clergy' not to suffer their offspring 'to be promoted in their churches, nor ... to marry their daughters to barons, or make their son barons out of the patrimony of Christ'.[14] These customs had become a veritable scandal, but the findings of the Council were futile. Although Archbishop Hamilton, who presided, was described as 'the venerable and most reverend father in Christ, and lord ... Primate of the whole realm of Scotland' he had as evil a record in regard to morality as his predecessor, Cardinal Beaton. Of the six bishops who attended, three were notoriously licentious, and there is no

---

13.   David Patrick, *Statutes of the Scottish Church*, p. 84.

14.   David Patrick, *op. cit.*, p. 92.

reason to believe that the lesser clergy were any better. The result was that the findings of the Council as to morality were disregarded.

Patronage

The vile system of patronage which had existed for three centuries did much to ruin the pre-Reformation Church. The pope, the king, the nobles and, in certain cases within their dioceses, the bishops all claimed the right to make appointments to benefices. The pope claimed the lion's share and caused intense discontent. In spite of interventions by Parliament (particularly in 1496), he went on making appointments to bishoprics and abbacies and to many vacant benefices, always in return for large money payments. There were sore complaints that the Vatican was draining the country of its financial resources.[15]

The patrons, of all kinds, often appointed most unsuitable persons. Frequently they were not ordained and were quite unfitted in character, and it was common for babes to be appointed. The manner in which James V secured the highest ecclesiastical offices for his infant illegitimate children shows how the evil system worked. Six of these children, some at the age of six, some at the age of seven, were appointed to certain of the richest ecclesiastical posts in Scotland from which enormous revenues were derived. Thus, James (the elder) became Commendator of the great abbey of Kelso in 1535 when aged six, and in 1541 was also made Abbot of Melrose. Few nobles in the land had such an income as this infant.

Abbacies and priories were given in commendam, i.e. in trust. The commendator was often a man of the world with no interest whatever in the salvation of souls. He drew the greater part of

---

15. *Acts of Parliament of Scotland* (year 1496), II, p. 238.

the rich revenues, and appointed some second-rate clergyman at a miserable pittance to do the spiritual work. It is not surprising that it was often badly done. Closely allied with this abuse was the system of pluralities whereby a man (quite frequently a layman) could hold a number of lucrative ecclesiastical offices for which he did no work. Professor John Cunningham well described this dreadful system: 'The great dignitaries of the Church set the example, and beside their bishoprics, held abbacies, priories, and parishes, for the sake of their revenues. Archbishop Forman and Cardinal Beaton were notorious for this. Everyone grasped as many livings as he could; and if the teinds were got hold of there was little thought for the cure of souls.'[16]

The same glaring evil existed in regard to monasteries. Very often the religious houses possessed anything from twenty-five to over thirty parishes with the teinds, rights of patronage, and other sources of revenue. These religious houses took the revenues and appointed a vicar in each parish to do the work at a wretched salary. These men were to be pitied. They were in poverty and the whole status of the parish priests was lowered, while the income and ecclesiastical dues 'went to fatten the useless inmates of some distant monastery'.[17] Some of the ablest and staunchest Roman Catholic historians have emphatically condemned these abuses connected with appointments to benefices. They recognize that they had a disastrous effect upon the Church.

The facts briefly referred to in this chapter give some idea as to how desperately reform was needed, and show also how lamentably the Roman Church had failed to institute any adequate reform. Men like Luther, Calvin and Knox had to arise before a real Reformation could be produced.

---

16.   John Cunningham, *Church History of Scotland*, 1, p. 205.
17.   *Op. cit.*, p.205

2

PIONEERS AND MARTYRS

It is virtually impossible to tell the exact moment when the seeds of the Reformation began to germinate in any particular country. There never was a time in which at least some independent spirits were not opposed to the Roman Church. This is seen in the story of the many sects which fought their battle for centuries on the continent and elsewhere, groups such as the Bogomils, Cathari, Albigenses, and Waldenses. Not a few – Marsilius of Padua (1270-1342) for example – contended from within against the policy and practices of the Roman Church, and held almost pure Protestant doctrine centuries before the Reformation. There was often a ferment of evangelical ideas going on secretly. This explains why the pope in 1329 ordered the bishops, when crowning kings in Scotland, to exact an oath that they would strive to root out those whom he called heretics. Clearly, not all were obedient to Roman Catholic teaching.

The *Lollards*, as the followers of John Wyclif (c. 1324-1384) were called, exercised much influence in the west of Scotland. Wyclif based his message solidly upon the Word of God long before Luther's day. He denied papal infallibility in matters of faith, rejected auricular confession, criticized belief in purgatory, pilgrimages, worship of saints, veneration of relics, and all else not based on biblical authority. Such were the tenets which the Lollards must have popularized in Aryshire and elsewhere when, after the death of Wyclif, many fled from England because of persecution. When the Council-General appointed the Duke of Rothesay Lieutenant to his father, Robert III, they charged him specially to restrain 'the cursit men, heretikis' who had been condemned by the Church. Wyntoun, the chronicler, declares of the Duke of Albany, who became governor of the kingdom in 1406:

> 'He was a constant Catholike;
> All Lollard he hated and heretike.'

This was 154 years before the Reformation, and yet, even then, the Lollard teachings were obviously causing concern.

So important did Walter Bower consider the burning of James Resby, one of these Lollards, who suffered at Perth in 1407, that he devoted a whole chapter to the matter in his continuation of Fordun's *Scotichronicon*. Resby was condemned by an ecclesiastical council presided over by the notorious Laurence of Lindores, 'inquisitor of heretical pravity,' the very existence of such an office showing that heresy had become serious. The worst charges against him were that he denied, first, that the pope was Christ's vicar on earth, and second, that a man of wicked life could be Christ's vicar. Bower laments that the same heresies persisted even after the burning of Resby.

The growing power of the Lollards is proved by the fact that in 1416 the University of St Andrews required of all receiving the degree of M.A. that they should swear that they would resist all Lollards. On 12 March 1425 Parliament decreed that each bishop should make inquisition as to 'heretikis and Lollardis' so that they could be punished. The teachings of Wyclif were carried by students from Oxford to Bohemia where they mightily influenced John Hus and Jerome of Prague. Paul Craw, a physician from Bohemia, came to Scotland to propagate these ideas. He was arrested in 1433 and condemned at the instigation of Laurence of Lindores, the inquisitor, and burnt at St Andrews. He was accused of denying transubstantiation, purgatory, the efficacy of absolution, and of urging that the Bible be given to the people in their own language. To prevent his professing and defending his faith before the people, a ball of brass was placed in his mouth at his martyrdom.[1] In 1494 thirty Lollards were arraigned before King James IV at Glasgow. Among other things charged against them by Archbishop Blackadder was that they denied that images should be worshipped, that relics of saints should be adored, that the bread and wine are changed into the body and blood of Christ in the Mass, and that the pope is the successor of Peter. Had it not been for the strenuous intervention of the king, who granted them a free pardon, they also would probably have been sent to the stake.[2] King James had several personal friends among the accused and this saved them all.

In spite of all the fulminations and hatred of men like Laurence of Lindores, the cause for which Resby and Craw died went continuously forward. This is proved by the fact that as early as 1543 the Scottish Parliament legalized the reading of the Scriptures in the vernacular. This was an event of vast importance, for it is to the study of the Bible that the Scots owe their robust faith and democratic principles. They learned there that neither king nor pope was head of the Church but

1.   John Knox, *History*, I, p. 7.

2.   *Op. cit.*, pp. 8-11.

Christ alone. This explains their attitude at the Reformation in 1560, and in the great Covenanting struggle in the 17th century. Few Scots have adequately realized their debt to the Lollards in preparing, during two centuries, the way for the Reformation.

Many Scottish students studied in continental universities, especially Paris, and not a few brought back the views of John Hus, which were then much discussed in centres of learning. As soon as Luther started his great movement in 1517, evangelical books and pamphlets began to infiltrate into Scotland and England often through Scottish ports, in spite of all that Church and Parliament could do. Tyndale's English translation of the New Testament came to have a marked influence when thus smuggled into the country. In 1525 and 1527 Parliament passed Acts to keep Scotland clean of what they called 'all sic filthe and vice' and threatened imprisonment and forfeiture of goods against any who should bring in the works of Luther. Notwithstanding this, the people were deeply stirred; the tide rose strongly against the abuses in the Church, and a chorus of criticism resounded throughout the land. In the words of Professor John Cunningham: 'Poets were not afraid to lampoon the idle monks and friars; wits perpetrated jokes at the expense of the voluptuous bishops; and even the rustics, when they met at the alehouse, told scandalous stories about the parish priest, some concubine he kept, or some good-looking woman he had inveigled at confession.' [3]

In the Church itself there were good-hearted priests and monks, and men of honest minds, who gladly accepted the truth when presented to them. The Reformation began

---

3. J.C. Cunningham, *Church History of Scotland*, 1, p. 166.

among this class. From inside the Roman Church came the first leaders and early martyrs of the Protestant cause. One of the noblest of these was Patrick Hamilton, son of Sir Patrick Hamilton of Kincavel, who was closely related by blood to the royal family and to the powerful House of Hamilton. After graduating with distinction at the University of Paris, where he may have heard the lectures of John Major, the great Scottish humanist, he proceeded to Louvain where he fell under the spell of Erasmus and distinguished himself in philosophy and languages. Returning to Scotland he became a member of the Faculty of Arts in St Andrews in October 1524. He began to speak freely of the new religious ideas he had heard discussed so often in continental centres of learning. He was also very diligent in circulating the New Testament and expounding it when in 1526 Archbishop James Beaton had to flee from St Andrews for political reasons. On his return, the Archbishop summoned him and accused him of heresy. On the advice of friends, he sought refuge again on the continent.

At Marburg University, a great centre of evangelicalism, Patrick Hamilton showed marked zeal and ability, publishing a series of doctrinal theses in Latin. These were the original of the invaluable little book known as *Patrick's Places*[4]. This is the earliest doctrinal production of the Scottish Reformation. It is deeply evangelical, plain, and pithy. Following St Paul, he taught that Christ alone can save, and that we must believe in the riches of His pardoning mercy and in the efficacy of His atoning death, and the freeness of His grace. It is this that saves, all the Reformers taught, not the frigid ecclesiastical legalism of the Middle Ages, or the carefully performed penance, or the prayers to the saints and martyrs.

---

4.   John Knox, *History*, II, p. 219 (Appendix).

In the late autumn of 1527 Master Patrick returned to Scotland determined to proclaim the gospel even if it cost him his life. With the basest treachery, Archbishop Beaton inveigled him across to Fife so as to get him away from the powerful protection of his relatives. He was invited to enter into friendly conference with leading churchmen and to talk freely of the reform of the Church, all pretending to be his friends. Notes were taken and he was arrested on 27 February 1528. Next day he was put on trial as a heretic, and was led to the stake at noon carrying his much-loved Bible in his hand. The arrangements had been made hastily and carelessly. The faggots were damp and slow to kindle, and so for six hours he suffered torments. He gave his gown and another garment to his servant saying that was all he could leave him except 'the example of his death'. Alexander Alesius, who was an eye-witness, wrote that 'the martyr never gave one sign of impatience or anger, nor ever called to heaven for vengeance on his persecutors, so great was his faith, so strong his confidence in God.'[5] The effect of his death was immense. Many felt that this treatment of a blameless young man was outrageous, especially as so many of the clergy were not punished even when leading vicious lives. A wise friend said to the archbishop: 'My Lord, if ye burn any more, except ye follow my counsel, ye will destroy yourselves. If ye will burn them, let them be burnt in how cellars; for the reik [i.e. smoke] of Maister Patrik Hammylton has infected as many as it blew upon.'[6]

The persecution, however, continued unabated for years. To abjure the doctrines of Master Patrick became a touchstone of orthodoxy. For refusing to do so Henry Forrest, who was

---

5.   Peter Lorimer, *Memoirs of Hamilton*, p. 155.

6.   John Knox, *History*, I, p. 18. 'how cellars' = low cellars.

in minor orders, was burnt at St Andrews about 1533 after bearing a heroic and unflinching testimony. Among those who fled the country was Alexander Alane (or Alesius), canon of the Augustinian Priory at St Andrews. He had tried his utmost at first to persuade Patrick Hamilton to abandon his evangelical views. Instead, he himself was converted to the Protestant faith. He was held in high honour by scholars in Germany, France and Switzerland, including Melanchthon and Theodore Beza. He became a distinguished professor of theology, but never returned to Scotland. Others who went overseas were Gavin Logie, principal regent at St Leonard's Collegeto which he gave a decided Lutheran bent, the illustrious classical scholar, George Buchanan, and the cultured and gentle George Wishart, the future martyr.

Constant search was made during this period for those having New Testaments or Lutheran books. In 1534 King James V and Cardinal Beaton presided over a great assize at Holyrood. Sixteen were sentenced to severe punishment including the forfeiture of their property. Norman Gourlay and David Stratoun were burnt at Greenside on the northern slope of the Calton Hill, 'according to the mercy of the papistical Kirk'.[7] Gourlay had been abroad and had imbibed Reformed ideas. These he abjured and was apparently burnt 'for the greater crime of having a wife, he being a priest'. [8]

━━⟡━━

Between the death of Patrick Hamilton and the Reformation about twenty were burnt at the stake. Many escaped to England and the continent; a large number suffered forfeiture of goods and

7.   John Knox, *History*, I, pp. 24-5.

8.   A.F. Mitchell, *Scottish Reformation*, pp. 38, 39. Cf. Lindsay of Pitscottie, *History* (1778), p. 236.

cruel imprisonment; a few recanted. After Hamilton, the most outstanding pre-Reformation martyr in Scotland was George Wishart, son of Sir James Wishart of Pitarrow in the Mearns. Born about 1513, he studied in King's College, Aberdeen, and fell under the influence of Erasmus through the Principal, Hector Boece. He became one of the best Greek scholars in Britain. For teaching his pupils in Montrose Academy to read the Greek New Testament, he was charged with heresy and fled to Bristol where he was befriended by Bishop Latimer in 1538. After this he studied at the best centres of learning in Germany and Switzerland, and brought back with him to Scotland the First Helvetic Confession. In 1542 he enrolled in Corpus Christi College, Cambridge. One of his students described him as 'a man of tall stature ... black haired, long bearded, comely of personage, well spoken after his country of Scotland, courteous, lowly, lovely, glad to teach, desirous to learn and well travelled.'[9] His death is most honourably commemorated on one of the windows of Corpus Christi College.

Some have asserted that he was involved about this time in a plot to murder Cardinal Beaton. The Earl of Hertford did refer to 'a Scottish man called Wishart' who was employed to carry messages from the conspirators to the English court. There were, however, many Wisharts in Scotland, and there is no evidence to show that this man was George Wishart. It is significant that no such charge was made against him in his lifetime, even by his bitterest enemies. It is, in fact, inconceivable that a man of his gentle ways and generous character should be a party to such a conspiracy.

George Wishart was a fervent preacher and loved to address the multitudes in the open air. On his return to Scotland he

9.   Emery Tilney; quoted in Cattley's *Foxe*, p. 626.

introduced the system of Bible exposition, or lecturing on passages of Scripture, which later became so popular and helpful. He was particularly fond of lecturing on the Epistle to the Romans, on which Calvin had recently written a commentary. His favourite centres of evangelization were Dundee, sometimes referred to then as 'the Geneva of Scotland', and Montrose, where he had formerly been a teacher. The magistrates of Dundee ordered him out of the town and reminded him that he was subject to arrest at any moment. Thereupon he went to Ayr where he had great success in spite of much opposition. Whether preaching from the steps of the market cross as at Ayr, or from a 'dry-stone dyke' as on the moor at Mauchline, he was heard attentively by crowds, so that through him the Word of God 'had free course and was glorified'.

In spite of his previous expulsion Wishart hurried back to Dundee when he heard that the plague had broken out there. His faithful ministration of the Word to believers and unbelievers brought unspeakable comfort to many. Not seldom the dying received the peace of God through faith in Christ's finished work. In spite of perils from the plague itself, he went on with the great work of ministering to soul and body. Later he preached at many places in East Lothian in spite of being in great danger. His successes in Angus had roused his foes to fury, and his friends had to move him from place to place for safety.

At this time there appears suddenly on the scene the man who was destined to do more for the Reformation in Scotland than any other. This was John Knox, a priest of the Roman Church, who was then serving as tutor at Longniddry House some miles from Edinburgh. Very little is known of his previous history, but ever since Wishart had come to East Lothian, he had accompanied him carrying a two-handed sword with which to defend him. When Wishart was leaving Haddington, Knox wanted to go with him but was told, 'Nay, return to your bairns [i.e. his pupils], and God bless you! One is sufficient for a sacrifice'. That night at Ormiston House, Wishart was handed over to the Earl of Bothwell under a solemn promise that he would not deliver him to the cardinal. The promise was broken and Wishart was committed to the dreadful 'bottle' dungeon in St Andrews Castle. On 28 February 1546 he was subjected to what was virtually a mock trial and was insulted and spat upon. The accusations against him were on the usual lines: obstinate heresy, denying auricular confession, purgatory, the Mass, and so on. Although the Regent Arran had warned Cardinal Beaton not to put Wishart to death until he had time to examine the case, the proud ecclesiastic on his own responsibility had him burnt on 1 March 1546 in spite of the murmured hostility of the people. The pile was placed in front of the Castle, and the cannons of the stronghold were trained on it to prevent the possibility of a rescue. It has been constantly reported that the cardinal and his friends reposed on luxurious cushions on a balcony gloating over the sufferings of their victim.

In spite of the rope round his neck and the chain round his waist, the brave martyr bore himself with dignity and constancy. He declared that he was suffering for the true gospel and for Christ's sake, and urged his hearers to be ever loyal to Christ whatever persecution might arise. His faith never faltered amid his sufferings, and he declared that that very night his soul would sup with his Saviour before the hour of six. He forgave all his enemies and earnestly prayed for them. The executioner was deeply moved and asked forgiveness. Wishart kissed his cheek saying, 'Lo! Here is a token that I forgive thee: my heart, do thine office'. After suffering in the fire for a time he was put upon the gibbet and hanged and then burned to powder. His death produced mourning among many and a sense of intense indignation arose against those responsible for the deed. He did not die in vain, for his sufferings did much to awaken the masses to the need for Reformation.

～※～

One of the greatest mistakes ever committed by the leaders of the Roman Catholic Church in Scotland was the burning twelve years later, in March 1558, of Walter Myln, at one time priest of Lunan, near Forfar. He was eighty-two years of age, and when brought before the ecclesiastical court was so infirm that he could scarcely stand. He was convicted of heresy and adjudged worthy of death, but so great was the sympathy felt for the heroic old saint that no magistrate could be got to pronounce sentence, until a disreputable minion of the archbishop did so. As the martyr was being led to the stake, his great age and tottering steps deeply stirred the multitude of onlookers. Overcoming all physical weakness and pain, he declared from the flames, 'I am fourscore and two years old, and could not live long by the course of nature; but a hundred better shall arise out of the ashes of my bones.'

It has been truly said that his death rang the knell of the papacy in Scotland. It is a great testimony to the power of the gospel that men such as Patrick Hamilton, George Wishart, and Walter Myln, reared in the bosom of the Roman Church, should be so transformed by the new light that they were willing to die for what they now saw to be the true faith.

3

CONFLICT BETWEEN
ENGLAND AND FRANCE

Although the Reformation in Scotland was essentially a religious movement, and in this respect different from that brought about by Henry VIII in England, we cannot understand its growth and development without looking at the political factors which governed the relationships of England, France and Scotland during this period.

James V became king in 1513 at the age of seventeen months, when his father, James IV, was killed on the fateful field of Flodden. In his will the late king appointed his queen, Margaret, a sister of Henry VIII, as regent. But the Scottish Parliament set this aside and, instead, called back from France the Duke of Albany, a cousin of James IV who had lived many years in exile in that country like his father before him. He was a friend of the French king, an Admiral of France, held vast territories there, and was infinitely more French than Scottish in his outlook. There was, however, a party which favoured the Dowager Queen Margaret. They organized armed opposition, but were defeated by Albany in battle. Thus Scotland became, officially, strongly pro-French.

Henry VIII, the uncle of the infant James V, was most anxious to secure a friendly understanding with Scotland because of the

growing power of France and the immense strength of the Emperor
Charles V. He realized that, in her somewhat isolated position,
and at a time when international relationships were difficult, an
alliance with the Scots would have been invaluable to England.
With incredible lack of wisdom, however, he attacked Scotland in
order to force her into an alliance, and his army destroyed some
Scottish towns. The result, of course, was that the Scots had to rely
on the French even more than before, and this in spite of a growing
irritation with their dictatorial methods. Henry VIII had a bullying
attitude to Scotland all his days. His ravaging of southern Scotland
with fire and sword a second time was not calculated to promote
the friendly relations he wanted. French aims were not more lofty
morally than those of Henry, and it suited them to keep Scotland
at enmity with England. On two occasions the regent, seeking to
serve France rather than Scotland, led a strong army to the English
border, but his nobles refused to invade England without cause.

The Queen Dowager had married the Earl of Angus, head
of the Red Douglases. There was a constant feud between his
house and that of the Hamiltons, both striving for supremacy
in the country's affairs. With French troops, and using
unrelenting French methods, Albany put down the strife and
shipped Angus off to France where he was kept under strict
surveillance. Nevertheless, he and his wife managed to escape
to England where Henry VIII gladly used them as the focal
point for gathering together Scottish nobles prepared to serve
the English interest in Scotland.

In 1523 Albany retired from Scotland. He had succeeded
in making the French alliance very unpopular, for the Scots
felt they had been used as pawns in that country's political
game. James V now began to govern at the age of twelve, with
Margaret, the Queen Dowager, as the real ruler, helped by
a regency council of which Arran was chief.

In 1534 Henry VIII broke with the pope because he could not get a divorce from Catherine of Aragon. The two Houses of Convocation issued a declaration that 'the Roman Pontiff has no greater jurisdiction bestowed on him by God in the Holy Scriptures than any other foreign bishop'. Although this was an event of far reaching importance, the manner in which Henry began the Reformation in England was far from satisfactory. Spiritually and doctrinally the Church remained virtually the same as before except that the sovereign, not the pope, was now its earthly head. In the hearts of the English people, however, a strong desire for reform was latent. The teachings of Luther and the Swiss Reformers were percolating into the country and the Reformation was bound to come, divorce or no divorce. But the country had to wait until the days of Edward VI, Henry's son, before seeing the Church of England placed on a true Protestant foundation.

As Henry VIII had many enemies on the continent, he sent Sir Ralph Sadler, an experienced statesman, to Scotland in 1537 to try to arrange an alliance with his nephew, who was now twenty-five years old. But James was about to marry a French princess, and so was virtually committed to a policy of hostility to England. Sadler assured him of the friendly feelings of Henry VIII, and besought him to use his intelligence in the matter of religion and not to be misled by the slanderous misrepresentations of the pope's emissaries. The English king strongly urged James to take possession of the monasteries and their vast wealth as had been done in England, and so solve his financial difficulties. Sadler also tried to turn James against Cardinal Beaton who had immense power and was pressing for the persecution of so-called heretics. But although James could, at times, mercilessly lash the prelates and priests for their sins, and severely threaten them, he remained loyal to the

Roman Church. Much of this loyalty was of a sordid nature, for he had secured from the pope, as we have seen, the appointment of his many bastard children to some of the wealthiest abbacies and priories in the kingdom while they were still infants. He himself could draw the revenues until they came of age.

Sadler persuaded James to agree to meet his uncle at York to discuss the future of their respective countries. He failed to keep his appointment, however, although Henry waited six days for him. His non-appearance was probably due to the interference of the hierarchy; but it is certain also that Henry himself was not acting in a straightforward manner. There were rumours of sinister plots to capture both the Scottish king and Cardinal Beaton. The English king was mortally offended.

On the death of his first queen, the daughter of the illustrious Francis I of France, a few months after their marriage, James married within a year Mary of Lorraine, daughter of the Duke of Guise. The man who was principally entrusted with making arrangements for this second marriage was Cardinal Beaton,[1] a great favourite with the French king, and already Bishop of Mirepoix in that country merely for the purpose of drawing the revenues. His great influence was strongly cast in the direction of making King James an enemy of England, and a champion of the French alliance, which would bring about also complete subservience to the Vatican. This is what one would expect, in any case, from the Scottish king's matrimonial connection with the House of Guise, which had a dreadful record for the persecution of heretics. James was so influenced that he persuaded Parliament to make it a crime punishable by death to argue against, or impugn, the pope's authority.

---

1.   See pp. 42, 43, 47-50.

After the failure of Sadler's diplomatic mission, war followed in 1542. The Duke of Norfolk reached the border with 40,000 men, but a small Scottish force under the Earl of Huntly gained a complete victory over a much larger English army at Hadden-Rig, an event which made the Scottish bishops wildly and foolishly rejoice. The Duke of Norfolk ravaged several border counties, but decided to withdraw southwards as winter was approaching. King James had 36,000 good troops with him on Fala Moor. The way to England was open and the Scots had an excellent opportunity to take revenge, but once more the nobles refused to advance. They declared that their obligations lay in defence, and stopped short of aggression beyond the national bounds. Underlying their decision was a desire to retaliate upon the king because he had associated too closely with the prelates, and had discarded the counsel of his nobles.

From now on the king was more than ever dependent on the hierarchy. He appealed to Cardinal Beaton and the other clerical leaders to form an army from the vassals on the Church lands to invade England secretly without the knowledge of the nobles. The result was the horrible fiasco of Solway Moss when the army of King James suffered a most humiliating defeat at the hands of a small English force. Many Scots were lost in the marshes, and 1,200 were taken prisoner. Among these were a number of earls, barons and gentlemen, whom Henry VIII treated well. They afterwards proved invaluable in forming a party in favour of an English alliance against the pro-French and pro-Vatican attitude of the Scottish court and the prelates.

The disaster of Solway Moss broke the heart of King James. In bitter grief, and with an overwhelming feeling that death was near, he sought the quietness of Falkland Palace in Fife. Nothing could relieve his misery. When a messenger arrived to tell him that the queen had borne a daughter at Linlithgow Palace, he impatiently exclaimed: 'It will end as it began; it came with a lass and it will end with a lass,' referring to the way the throne came to the Stewarts. He had been strong and brave and yet died at the age of thirty-one on 13 December 1542. His baby daughter, Mary, now became queen at the age of one week. She was destined to live through tumultuous days and to stir the hearts of many, but to end in tragedy.

Immediately Henry VIII of England heard of the death of the Scottish king, he began overtures for the marriage of the infant queen to his only son, Edward. The Scottish nobles welcomed the idea but the incredibly domineering and dictatorial attitude of Henry ruined everything. Cardinal Beaton produced a document purporting to be a will of James V appointing him governor of Scotland with Argyll, Moray and Huntly as a Council. The proud nobles of Scotland treated the document as a forgery and removed Beaton from the regency, his place being taken by the Earl of Arran, next heir to the throne, on 22 December 1542. This step was widely approved, but it roused the Cardinal to more opposition than ever to the Reformation. Posing as a great Scottish patriot, although more a Frenchman than a Scotsman, he denounced the proposed alliance with England and sought men, arms and money from the House of Guise to retain Scotland in the faith of Rome and in alliance with France.[2] The easy-going and changeable Earl of Arran was strengthened in his opposition to Beaton by the arrival from England of the Earl of Angus and other prominent Douglases who had been long in exile.[3] With them

---

2. Sadler's *State Papers*, I, p. 138.

3. See p. 40.

came Glencairn, Maxwell, Somerville, Fleming and Oliphant, who, to secure their liberty from Henry VIII, swore to work for a treaty which would provide for the marriage of the infant Queen Mary to Prince Edward, and for the handing over of the child immediately to the English court. The principal fortresses of Scotland were also to be delivered to Henry.

This unpatriotic surrender played into the hands of the cardinal, and these nobles were discredited. On 12 March 1543, however, the Three Estates (i.e. Parliament) agreed cordially to the marriage, but resolved emphatically that the young queen should not go to England until she was ten years of age, and that not a single fortress should be entrusted to Henry VIII. The independence of the country must be maintained at all costs both before and after the marriage. Henry fumed and threatened and declared he would compel the Scots to deliver their queen into his keeping. He caused most bitter indignation by raising the old demand of Edward I to be recognized as Lord Paramount of Scotland with the government of that country entirely under his authority.

Henry's intransigence completely suited the policy of Cardinal Beaton and the pro-French party. The return from France of John Hamilton, Abbot of Paisley, illegitimate brother of the governor, also fitted well into their plans. The cardinal and the abbot played their part skilfully and worked up a fierce hostility against England among the common people. It was too much for the timid and fickle governor. Although regarded as a great hope of the Protestant cause, he now became its enemy. He dismissed his chaplains of the Reformed faith, John Rough and Thomas Williams. This was followed by his reconciliation with the cardinal, the doing of penance at Stirling, and his reception once more into the Roman Church.

Although Arran had previously put Beaton in prison, the latter now became the real governor of Scotland. Bitter persecution followed, culminating in the burning of George Wishart at St Andrews on 1 March 1546,[4] after five persons had been brutally martyred at Perth. The cardinal secured control of the person of the infant sovereign and removed her to Stirling, and got Parliament to annul the arrangements for the marriage with the English prince, Edward, although by now favourable treaties had been signed. Henry VIII in his fury resolved 'to seek Mary of Scotland for his son, with a word in his hand – a bad way to woo a woman'.[5] He seized many Scottish ships, and ravaged the country from Berwick to Edinburgh, the possessions of friends (for example, the lands of the Earl of Angus) and foes being attacked indiscriminately. Edinburgh and Leith were plundered and the fires burnt for three days. Even the friends of the English alliance were alienated by Henry's actions. Arran and the cardinal fled in terror to Linlithgow.

Although the Scots gained a brilliant victory at Ancrum Moor in 1545, the English under Hertford burnt all the crops in the eastern part of the borders that same year. Seven monasteries and other religious houses were destroyed including the beautiful abbeys of Kelso, Melrose, Dryburgh, Jedburgh and Eccles. Five towns and 240 villages were given to the flames.

Henry VIII died on 28 January 1547, but Hertford (now Lord Protector Somerset) continued to attack Scotland. At Pinkie Cleuch, near Inveresk, he gained a crushing victory. It was a humiliating defeat for the Scots, but Somerset failed to follow it up and returned home. The English were now

---

4. See pp. 31-35

5. J. Cunningham, *Church History of Scotland*, I, p. 184.

hated more than ever and Scotland became even more united to France. On the advice of Mary of Lorraine and D'Oysel, the French military representative, it was resolved to send the young queen to France and have her married to the Dauphin. Henry II of France rejoiced and sent 5,000 of his troops into Scotland. Mary, aged six, sailed for France on 7 August 1548. The French king spoke as if Scotland were already part of his country, the very result which Henry VIII and Somerset had so much desired to avoid. Had it not been for their intolerable intransigence the alliance would have been with England, not France, and the union of the crowns would have been greatly hastened. It would have saved both lands from much sorrow and bloodshed.

Some have argued that it would have been a betrayal of their country for the Scots to have entered at that time into an alliance with England; but Henry VIII and the French rulers were about equally unscrupulous. They were only interested in using Scotland for their own purposes, and the evidence shows that they were quite prepared to act treacherously when they thought it would help their own cause. Their aims were, in fact, identical – to annex Scotland and make it a province of their own country. It was, therefore, no more patriotic to be allied to the one rather than to the other. When finally, the alliance with England was cemented in the days of Queen Elizabeth, the situation had greatly changed, and the interests of the two countries, both of them now Protestant nations, clamoured for united action.

4

THREEFOLD CRISIS

AT ST ANDREWS

During the years of his primacy from 1539 to 1546, Cardinal Beaton[1] was chiefly responsible for the cruel persecutions and martyrdoms which took place. In the words of Froude, 'His scent of heresy was as the sleuth-hound's, and as the sleuth-hound's, was only satisfied with blood'. He was, however, a man of marked ability and boundless energy, and possessed many of the qualities of a great statesman. He had had much success in the diplomatic service, but his long residence in France had made him 'three parts French'. He so loved the scholars and nobles of that country that he 'determined to imitate their ways even down to their scandalous laxity of morals and merciless treatment of so-called heretics'.[2] His diplomacy was successful in persuading James V not to follow the example of his uncle Henry VIII in sequestrating the abbeys and monasteries. Although well aware of the failings of churchmen, the blandishments of Sadler, Henry's emissary, had no effect on the king. Pope Paul III saw clearly the value

---

1.   See pp. 40, 42.

2.   A.F. Mitchell, *The Scottish Reformation* (Baird Lecture, 1899), p. 47.

of Beaton in regard to such issues and so made him a cardinal. Merle D'Aubigné writes of him: 'He was a hierarchical fanatic. Two points, above all, were offensive to him in evangelical Christians: one, that they were not submissive to the pope; the other, that they censured immorality in the clergy, for his own licentiousness drew on himself similar rebukes. He aimed at being in Scotland a kind of Wolsey, only with more violence and bloodshed'.[3]

First Crisis

It is not surprising that this ruthless man, with his vaulting ambition and dominating personality, should have provoked enmities. Not only his evil record as a persecutor, but his political activities, made him deeply hated in many quarters. This led to the conspiracy to murder him in his own castle of St Andrews. The conspirators were the two brothers Norman and John Leslie of Rothes, Fife; William Kirkcaldy of Grange; and James Melville of Carnbee. They entered the castle early in the morning of 29 May 1546 when the drawbridge was down to admit some workmen. There is no need to describe the scene of horror which ensued. They were deaf to the cardinal's pathetic pleas for mercy and despatched him with their swords with many wounds. The sensation caused throughout Scotland by this terrible deed could not have been greater.

It should be noted that it happened fourteen years before the Reformation, at a time when there was no organized Protestant Church in Scotland. The murderers were moved by feelings of personal pique and hatred against one whom they regarded as an enemy of the common weal. They never claimed to be worthy members of the Reformed Church.

3.   Merle D'Aubigné, *The Reformation in the Time of Calvin*, VI, p. 131.

None of us could defend for a moment such a dastardly deed. At the same time it must be remembered that Beaton was himself a cold-blooded persecutor whose personal life was far from exemplary. Sir David Lyndsay well summed up what many Scotsmen were thinking:

> 'As for the Cardinal, I grant
> He was the man we weel could want,
> And we'll forget him soon;
> And yet I think the sooth to say,
> Although the loon is weel away,
> The deed was foully done.' [4]

The death of the cardinal was a direct challenge to the Roman Church. Feelings were much embittered and for a time life became almost intolerable for those in sympathy with the Reformed cause. It was, however, the handwriting on the wall for the hierarchy in Scotland. The political power of the papacy was never quite the same again. St Andrews Castle was held by the insurgents and became a rallying ground for opponents of the Roman Church.

Some writers have sought to fasten on the whole Scottish people the obloquy of Beaton's murder. This is manifestly unfair. Such events have, unfortunately, not been uncommon. Think, for example, of the murder of Thomas à Becket of Canterbury, in the twelfth century and of Sudbury, Archbishop of York, in the thirteenth. Even popes have been slain at the hands of their own co-religionists.

Archbishop John Hamilton who succeeded Beaton as Primate, resembled his predecessor in his immoralities but was inferior in ability. This had its effect as the time of the Reformation drew near.

---

4.   Quoted by Thomas McCrie, *Sketches of Scottish Church History*, p. 43.

Second Crisis

Owing to the furore which arose over the death of the cardinal, many who cherished Reformed Church ideas sought refuge in St Andrews Castle. These were denounced as accursed by the new archbishop and declared rebels. Among them was John Knox, the friend of Wishart,[5] who ten months after Beaton's murder came to St Andrews, bringing with him for safety his young charges, Francis and George Douglas of Longniddry, and Alexander Cockburn, heir of the laird of Ormiston. Besides giving them the secular education appropriate to their years, he read to them a catechism and got them to repeat it publicly in St Andrews Parish Church. He also read and expounded to them the Gospel of John in the chapel of the castle. Thus, many came to know the truth as it is in Jesus. Some of the most discerning among the hearers, such as Henry Balnaves of Halhill (a cosmopolitan scholar and great lawyer) and John Rough (formerly a priest but now a Protestant preacher), noted his excellent doctrine and ability and began to urge him to become a preacher. He stoutly refused because 'he would not run where God had not called him'.

The congregation, however, were not to be balked of their desire. They arranged privately that John Rough should preach upon the right of a congregation to call to God's service any man in whom they espied divine gifts, and that he should stress how dangerous it was for him to refuse. Turning to Knox he charged him in the name of God and the congregation to take up this holy calling of public preaching. The congregation gave emphatic assent. John Knox, completely overcome, burst into tears and withdrew to his chamber. Greatly though this incident troubled him, it did not prevent him, not many days after,

---

5.   See p. 33.

from entering the lists in St Andrews Parish Church and con-
futing Dean John Annand who had harassed John Rough in his
preaching. It is worth noting that, while Knox was absolutely
fearless before men, his attitude before God was one of profound humility and reverence. Once he was satisfied that God
had called him he never flinched in declaring the truth of the
gospel to men. Yet so great was his sense of responsibility to the
most High that he almost trembled every time he ascended the
pulpit steps to declare the Lord's message.

The populace insisted that Knox should preach in the parish
church of St Andrews. Taking as his text Daniel 7:24-5,
he maintained that the papacy was the Antichrist foretold
in Scripture, and that the whole system of popes and priests
placed a barrier between man and God's original message.
He compared the scriptural doctrine of justification by faith,
which teaches that man is 'justified by faith only' and that 'the
blood of Jesus Christ purges us all from all our sins', with the
doctrine of the Roman Church which ascribes justification
to the works of the law, 'yea to the works of man's invention,
as pilgrimages, pardons, and other such baggage. That the
papistical laws repugned to the law of the Evangel, he proved
by the laws made of observation of days, abstaining from
meats, and from marriage, which Christ Jesus made free, and
the forbidding whereof Saint Paul called "the doctrine of
devils".[6] The effect of this address was prodigious. Some said,
'Others sned [i.e. lopped off] the branches of the Papistry,
but he strikes at the root to destroy the whole.' Others
declared, 'Master George Wishart spake never so plainly, and
yet he was burnt: even so will he be'[7]. Soon after, Knox was

6.   John Knox, *History*, I, p. 85.

7.   *Op. cit.*, I, p. 86.

called to a convention of the Greyfriars and Blackfriars of St Andrews presided over by John Wynram, the sub-prior. There he strongly maintained that all religion which is 'not commanded' of God, or which is 'invented' by men, even with the best motives, is wrong. This view was based on the First Helvetic Confession which had been brought to Scotland by George Wishart, and which became basic in the Reformed Church.[8] To Knox it was blasphemous to describe the pope as 'the successor of Peter', 'the Vicar of Christ', 'most blessed', or as one 'that cannot err'.

The call of Knox to be a preacher of the gospel constituted a crisis of the first magnitude in his own life and in the life of his country. It meant his frank and open entry into the service of his Master to preach and to champion His cause, no matter what the opposition might be. He himself insisted that he did not take up the task of guiding his people 'at his own hand, or accept it at his own leisure'. We shall not understand Knox's character and work if we forget that he felt himself called by God. Certainly, God had provided a man of grace, full of courage and force of character to fight a stern battle against ignorance, superstition and depravity. It would have been futile for any ordinary man to have assayed his task. Not only was there the shocking corruption which was destroying the spiritual life of the church, there was also the opposition of crafty and powerful enemies. The new religious movement needed a strong man to point it to higher ideals. Even in the garrison of St Andrews Castle there were some whose lives were a disgrace. In countless ways the powerful hand of Knox was needed to guide and strengthen, and his influence was speedily felt.

---

8.   John Knox, *History*, I, pp. 87-92.

Third Crisis

The Regent Arran had failed to subdue the garrison either by force or by cajolery. By the end of June 1547, however, twenty-one French galleys, under the command of the brilliant leader Leo Strozzi, succeeded, by skilful operations, in devastating the walls of the castle. On the last day of July the garrison was forced into surrender. Some of those captured, among them John Knox, were consigned as slaves to the galleys; the remainder were sent to prisons in France. During his nineteen months' slavery Knox must have suffered unutterable things. The only reference to the matter in his own writings was: 'How long I continued prisoner, what torments I sustained in the galleys, and what were the sobs of my heart, is now no time to recite'.[9] It is well known, however, how dreadfully such slaves suffered, perspiring at the oar even in the coldest weather, miserably fed, often ill and liable to be unmercifully whipped.

The capture of the castle by the French was the third great crisis at St Andrews in little over a year. Having extracted from the splendid old building treasure worth £100,000, the greater part of the noble pile was razed to the ground. Its capture, and the carrying into slavery of John Knox and other leaders, caused intense depression in Protestant circles. On the continent, too, the cause seemed virtually lost that year. The defeat of the Protestants by the Emperor at Mühlberg on 24 April 1547 was a staggering blow. The once powerful Protestant leaders, the Elector of Saxony and the Landgrave of Hesse, were now in chains. Through the *Interim Decree* the Emperor was suppressing congregations, and banishing or burning preachers. But John Knox, even in the galleys, refused

9.   John Knox, *History*, I, p. 182.

to be daunted. When one day, as they were sailing past, he discerned in the distance the towers of St Andrews, he expressed to a friend his absolute certainty that he would yet glorify God by preaching the gospel there once more. He testifies triumphantly to the unflinching steadfastness of his Scottish companions. 'Those that were in the galleys were threatened with torments if they would not give reverence to the Mass ... but they could never make the poorest of that company to give reverence to that idol.' When compulsion was applied to Knox to make him reverence a painted figure of our Lady, he cast it in the river saying, 'Let our Lady now save herself: she is light enough; let her learn to swim.'[10] It is remarkable that no amount of suffering could make these recent converts from the Roman Church prove disloyal to their new faith.

It seemed tragic that the work of reformation in Scotland should have been arrested by the carrying away captive of its leading figure. The hand of God, however, was in it. If the whole nation had suddenly embraced the Protestant faith it might well have led to shallowness and over-confidence. It was desirable that the people should have time to ponder well the truths which had been proclaimed among them. John Knox's hard experiences in the galleys, followed by ten years in exile, were to be an invaluable preparation for his life's work.[11] His outlook was thus broadened and he was freed from insularity, that common weakness of our island people. He secured a deep insight into the complexities and frailties of human character. He learned self-control, patience, and steadiness, and developed a character marked by calm self-possession. This served him well in facing dangers and difficulties in later days. On

10. John Knox, *op. cit.*, I, p. 108.

11. See also chapter 6.

the continent, he saw in a wider context the policy and plans of the Roman Church with its plots and intrigues. He saw also that, small as Scotland was, it was yet pivotal in the battle of the Reformation, for both France and Spain wished to have it as a jumping-off place to attack Protestant England.

In addition to all this, he had the immense privilege of friendship with Calvin, Bullinger, Beza, Melanchthon, Bucer, and other great continental leaders of the Reformation. His mind was sharpened and quickened as it could not possibly have been if he had remained in Scotland. He formed many contacts, and carried on a vast correspondence in later years, so that he was able to keep in touch with all the political and religious currents in Europe. In addition he knew the great Sir William Cecil (Lord Burghley) who had at his disposal all the resources of the English government.

We have anticipated a little, the course of events after the fall of St Andrews Castle in 1547, to show how, in the providence of God, what seemed an unmitigated disaster turned out to be for good and produced wonderful results. But at the time it was a most bitter experience for all who loved the Protestant cause and especially for those who suffered. It is a most striking fact, however, that no one thought of turning back, even when enduring the most cruel persecution. Neither at home, where the opposition was now very bitter, not amid the privations of the galleys and of exile, did the upholders of the Protestant cause flinch, nor did they show the slightest desire to abandon the struggle. They had found the truth and were determined to maintain it at all costs. Like an ancient writer, they felt that 'As for truth, it endureth, and is always strong; it liveth and conquereth for ever',[12] Although everything seemed

---

12.   I Esdras IV. 38

against them at the end of 1547, the Scottish Protestants at home and abroad were convinced that God's truth was worth suffering for and in that spirit they faced the great dangers which threatened.

5

SCOTLAND DURING THE DAYS OF KNOX'S EXILE

The capture of St Andrews Castle by the French in July 1547 with its serious consequences, and the victory of the English at Pinkie in September, had left the Scottish Protestants in a state of indescribable misery.[1] The garrisons then left in Scottish strongholds by the Protector Somerset were, moreover, soon driven out with the help of excellent French troops. With these soldiers stationed on their soil, and with their young queen living in France, the Scots were now very closely linked to their old friends, the French.

Very soon, however, they began to find that this alliance was as burdensome and unpleasant as would have been an alliance with their old enemies, the English. It is well known that even the governor, the Earl of Arran, and his brother, John Hamilton, the new Archbishop of St Andrews, supported the French alliance purely because of the force of circumstances. There was a growing number of nobles and others throughout the country who inclined more and more towards England. A facetious correspondent in Scotland, writing to the Protector Somerset, said of the governor's relationship to France that he was 'like one that holdeth a wolf by the ears, in doubt to hold and in danger to let go.'[2]

---

1.   Cf. pp. 44, 53.

2.   Hume Brown, *John Knox*, I, p. 273 (quoted from *Calendar of State Papers* (Scotland), 29 November 1548).

The causes of irritation were innumerable. Even the Queen Mother, Mary of Guise, although the ruling passion of her life was the maintenance of the French ascendancy and the strengthening of the Roman Church, wrote to her brothers, the Guise leaders, on 12 November 1549: 'In this connection it is needful that I should tell you that if the king does not issue some order to the cavalry which he has here, our country will be unable to endure the evils which the soldiery inflict ... They [i.e. the French soldiers] eject them from their houses, and have never paid a *liard* for the feeding of their horses.'[3] There were times when the Scots, in self-defence, resisted. On one occasion, for example, there was a fracas in the High Street of Edinburgh, which led to the death of the Provost, or Captain, of the castle, with six other citizens and a woman.[4] Naturally such conflicts between Scots and French caused much bad feeling. This partly explains why, in 1560, the Scots sought and obtained the help of England and drove out the French, thus opening the way for the official establishment of the Protestant Church.

Although these political happenings are important if we are to understand the steps leading up to the Reformation, the growth of Protestant sentiment from 1547 to 1559, the period during which John Knox was in the galleys and then in exile, is the most remarkable feature of all. When the Castle of St Andrews was captured by the French it seemed as if the cause of the Reformed Church was lost. Scotland was virtually governed by the French, and the Roman Church seemed permanently established. Indeed, throughout all Europe, the Protestant cause was at its lowest ebb. Yet the amazing fact

---

3. Hume Brown, *op. cit.*, I, p. 276.

4. John Knox, *Reformation in Scotland*, I, p. 105.

emerges that, at this very time when the Protestant movement in Scotland was without a leader, the Reformed doctrines took an ever-increasing hold upon all classes. Thus, when in 1555 John Knox returned from Geneva for a visit of a few months, he was overjoyed to find great masses of the people thirsting for the gospel. This he related in a letter to his mother-in-law, Mrs Bowes,[5] and declared that they were 'night and day sobbing and groaning for the bread of life. If I had not seen it with my own eyes in my own country, I could not have believed it. Depart I cannot until such time as God quench their thirst a little'.[6]

During his brief stay in the country he visited Edinburgh. There, as he preached in the house of James Sime, a citizen of considerable standing, some important persons waited on his ministry. Among the questions which arose was whether it was permissible to believe the gospel in secret and yet give an outward conformity to the Roman Church by countenancing the sacrifice of the Mass in accordance with the practice of that Church. The laird of Dun, John Erskine, whose noble character, winsomeness and wisdom provide inestimable value to the Protestant cause, arranged a supper party to discuss the question. Young William Maitland of Lethington, son of Sir Richard Maitland, was there with other doubters, not because he was a religious man but because of the curiosity which was aroused in a restless and brilliant mind by the novelty of a new creed. The subject seems to have been freely ventilated. Knox began by asserting with emphasis 'that no-eyise it was lauchfull to a Christiane to present him self to that idoll'[7] (the Mass). Some were anxious to temporize, for it was still dangerous to

5.   Cf. pp. 70

6.   David Laing, *Works of John Knox*, IV, pp. 217, 218.

7.   David Laing, *op.cit.*, I, p. 247.

take a strong stand against the teaching and practices of the Roman Church. In spite of the fact that Maitland was one of the ablest men of his age and a master in argument and diplomacy, Knox drove him and his friends from every refuge. Finally he confessed that Knox was right. 'I see perfectly,' said he, 'that our shifts will serve nothing before God, seeing that they stand us in so small stead before man.'[8] The decisions of this supper-party were far-reaching. They showed that the foundation truths of the Protestant faith were radically different from those of Rome, and that there could be no compromise between them. The priestcraft and magic associated with the altar and the Mass were brushed aside, and it was made abundantly clear that there could be no association with image worship, or anything savouring of idolatry.

Going from Edinburgh to Angus with John Erskine of Dun, Knox found in that county the same enthusiasm as in Edinburgh. He was 'daily exercised in doctrine, whereunto resorted the principal men of that country.'[9] Clearly the good seed sown by George Wishart in and around Montrose was now bearing a rich harvest.

At the house of another laird, Sir James Sandilands of Calder, West Lothian, who was one of the most honourable and eminent public figures in the country, John Knox found similar conditions prevailing. Among the many who waited on his ministry were Lord Erskine, Lord Lorn (afterwards Earl of Argyll) and Lord James Stewart, natural son of James V, who later became one of the great figures of the Reformation and is known as the Regent Moray. All three played a notable part in subsequent events. Their presence at Calder House would

8.   David Laing, *op.cit.*, I, pp. 247-9.

9.   *Op. cit.*, I, p. 249.

reveal clearly to Knox what a grip the Reformed doctrines were getting on the minds of good and thoughtful men. In the West also, in Ayrshire and Renfrewshire, John Knox found an equally strong, rising tide in favour of the Reformed cause. Among its unwavering supporters, for example, was that fervent lover of the truth, the Earl of Glencairn.

This remarkable movement was by no means confined to the upper classes. The common people in the West, where their grandparents had been deeply moved by the preaching of the Lollards, were now ready to rise in their thousands to defend the same cause. In Angus and the Mearns the teachings of George Wishart, far from being forgotten, were having a more vital effect than ever on the lives of the humbler classes.

Nothing could show more clearly the growing power and resolution of the Reformed party than the fact that when the authorities of the Roman Church summoned John Knox to Blackfriars Church, Edinburgh, to give an account of himself, he went accompanied by Erskine of Dun and 'diverse otheris gentlemen'. So strong was the demonstration in Knox's favour that the bishops did not put in appearance. So far was the Reformer from being judged by the hierarchy that for ten days in succession he preached in Edinburgh to greater gatherings than ever.[10]

While cultured writers, such as George Buchanan, were profoundly influencing the learned in favour of the Reformation, a remarkable impression was being produced upon the minds of ordinary folk by the plays, ballads, and pamphlets which, by this time, had become enormously popular throughout the country. As early as 2 June 1543 the Lords of Council were thoroughly alarmed by these, and ordained that

---

10.   David Laing, *op. cit.*, I, p. 251.

in view of the 'sclanderous billis, writtingis, ballatis and bukis' which were daily written and printed, no man should dare to make, write, or print any such matter under pain of death and confiscation of his goods.[11] We see that this enactment, like others of the same kind, had no effect, for the Provincial Council, six years later in 1549, enacted that 'Every ordinary shall diligently inquire within his own diocese what persons have in their keeping any books of rhymes or popular songs containing calumnies and slanders defamatory of churchmen and church institutions, or infamous libels, or any kind of heresy'. Those having such were to be proceeded against with the utmost rigours of the law. The flood of literature of this kind constantly increased in spite of the wild denunciations of irate churchmen. Parliament therefore returned to the attack by enacting on 1 February 1552 that no printer presume to print any books, ballads, songs, blasphemations, rhymes or tragedies, whether in Latin or English, until they had been passed by some 'discreet person' appointed by the bishops.[12]

Few original lyrics on sacred themes have been as popular as *The Gude and Godlie Ballates* prepared by the Wedderburn brothers of Dundee; James, John and Robert. They consisted of: first, a doctrinal section including a Catechism, the Creed, the Lord's Prayer, and the Ten Commandments, all in metre; second, versions of twenty-two metrical psalms, and some hymns; and third, secular songs converted into religious poetry. They were set to popular airs and were sung on Sundays and week days. They taught the Reformed doctrines and cast ridicule on popish teachings. It is safe to say they did infinitely more to popularize Protestant views than the most learned

11.   Joseph Robertson, *Statuta*, II, pp. 294, 295.

12.   *Acts of Parliament of Scotland*, II, pp. 488, 489.

theological tomes of the masters could ever have done! Here is Psalm Ii. I in the *Godlie Ballates*:

> Have mercy on me, O gude Lord,
> Efter thy greit mercie;
> My sinful life does me remord,
> Quhilk sair hes grevit Thee.

Here, again, is a condemnation of prayers to the saints:

> To pray to Peter, James and Johne,
> Our saulis[13] to saif, power haif they none,
> For that belongs to Christ alone,
> He deit[14] thairfore, He deit thairfore.

These ballads of the Wedderburns began to appear about 1542, and were, of course, in vernacular Scots. Besides the Wedderburns, there were very many others who wrote with varying degrees of success. The most outstanding of all was, undoubtedly, Sir David Lyndsay whose works appealed so powerfully to gentle and simple folk, from the throne downwards. In his writings such as the *Satyre of the Thrie Estaitis*, and *Kitteis Confessioun* he did much to shake faith in the Roman Church. His exposure of the vices of the clergy brought the Church into ridicule by

> 'The flash of that satiric rage,
> Which, bursting on the early stage,
> Branded the vices of the age,
> And broke the keys of Rome.'[15]

We would not seek to copy Lyndsay's rough and sometimes indelicate phraseology, but it was undoubtedly effective.

---

13.   saulis = souls.

14.   deit = died.

15.   Quoted by D. Hay Fleming, *Reformation in Scotland*, p. 182.

Over and above all this there was the fact that Parliament, on 15 March 1543, legalized the reading of the Holy Scriptures in English or Scots. This was a great step towards Reformation, for hitherto the Roman Church had done its best to prevent the reading of God's Word among the masses, and even among ecclesiastics it was usually known only in Latin. This action of the Estates in giving legal recognition to the right of every Scotsman to read the Bible in the vernacular was due to the influences which were then affecting an increasing number of the cultured classes in Scotland where, only now, was the Renaissance making a serious impression. The circulation of the Scriptures through Lutheran initiative was having its effect. In particular, William Tyndale's version of the English Bible was being widely circulated in England, and in 1537 Henry VIII had approved the publication of the Great Bible and ordered a copy to be placed in every parish church. Such an example was infectious, and do what they would, the hierarchy could not stop many copies of the Word of God from entering Scotland both from England and the continent.

Moreover, a great amount of Protestant doctrinal writings were coming into the country, and many students were constantly moving to and from the great centres of learning on the continent where they became familiar with the teachings of John Hus, Martin Luther, and other Reformers. The results are seen in the great output of Scottish literature exposing trenchantly the failings of the Roman Church as indicated above. This, in turn, affected an ever-widening circle. The intense revulsion caused in the popular mind by the martyrdoms which had taken place was another powerful factor influencing men's minds. The cumulative effect of all this was seen in a remarkable desire to read and study the Word of God. In the words of Knox, 'This was no small victory of Christ Jesus, fighting against the conjured enemies of his verity; no small comfort to such as before were held in such bondage that they durst not have read the Lord's Prayer, the Ten Commandments, nor articles of their faith, in the English tongue, but they should have been accused of heresy. Then might have been seen the Bible lying almost upon every gentleman's table'.[16]

The foregoing helps to explain how it was that John Knox, during his short visit to Scotland from 1555 to 1556, found among all classes such a thirst for the Word of Life. Although there were at this time scarcely any Protestant preachers in Scotland and the Reformed Church was not organized even in a rudimentary form, during this visit Knox found everywhere that amazing uprising in favour of the Reformed doctrines which we have already noticed. This is all the more striking when it is remembered that the constituted authorities, led by Mary of Lorraine, now Queen Regent, were hostile to the Protestant cause and it was still very perilous to maintain the Reformed doctrines, as is proved by the martyrdom of Walter Myln as late as 1558.[17]

One would have said that without strong leadership it would have been impossible for the Reformed cause to make headway against such formidable and determined opposition, yet its adherents continued to increase. This is clearly shown by such incidents as the destruction in 1558 of the image of St Giles, the patron saint of the city of Edinburgh. There had been growing opposition in the city to the veneration of images, and in the summer of that year a band of men secretly removed the large image from the church, drowned him in the Nor Loch and then burnt him. Archbishop Hamilton demanded that the

---

16. John Knox, *History*, I, p. 45.
17. Cf. p. 35.

magistrates and city council should either restore the image or provide a new one. They replied that, according to their understanding, God had ordered the destruction of images and idols. They requested the archbishop to show them from the Old Testament or the New, any warrant for making them. He enjoined them to obey under pain of excommunication, but the threat, once so overpowering, had now no effect on the city fathers.

A smaller St Giles had to be borrowed for the saint's celebration on 1 September. The Queen Regent led the procession and there was an imposing array of ecclesiastics, and many others of the faithful. The occasion was enlivened with tabors, trumpets, banners and bagpipes. When the Queen Regent went to dine, a group of Protestants obtained possession of the image. A great tumult ensued, but it is very apparent that the Protestants were in a big majority. The cry went up, 'Down with the idol; down with it', and one of the crowd took the saint 'by the heels, and dadding[18] his head to the calsay,[19] left Dagon without head or hands'. Chaos ensued; the ecclesiastics fled pell-mell leaving behind them, in their haste, crosses, surplices and caps, and 'happy was he who got first to his house'.[20]

An event of this kind shows how the masses were reacting to the abuses and corruptions which had so long disgraced the Church. Their actions may have been crude, but possibly no other method would have availed at a time when violence and oppression were the order of the day. The significant fact is that all this occurred during the years when John Knox was in

18. dadding = dashing.
19. calsay = causeway.
20. For a remarkably vivid account of this affray see John Knox, *Reformation in Scotland*, I, pp. 125-9.

exile from Scotland. In certain quarters the idea is sedulously propagated that the Reformation in Scotland was brought about by a wild and unscrupulous fanatic called John Knox who wickedly conspired against the Roman Church and lo! All the people followed him and violently destroyed the old Church. This is not what happened, for during the years of Knox's exile Protestant truth took possession of the hearts of men as we have already described. Far from being a sudden conspiracy organized by one man, the feeling of disgust with the Roman Church had reached breaking-point after generations of suffering. For the first time men had an open Bible in their hands, and the study of the gospel wrought a mighty change in their hearts and minds. The Reformation would have taken place even if John Knox had never returned to Scotland. A new spirit was at work and was fast taking possession of the nation. In the words of Dr Donald Maclean, echoing the view of Dr D. Hay Fleming, 'It was the Evangel that made the Reformation. It was the Evangel that gave the Reformation its power, stability and success; and it was the Evangel that furnished it with its defences'.[21]

---

21. Donald Maclean, *Counter-Reformation in Scotland*, p. 23.

6

KNOX IN ENGLAND AND ON THE CONTINENT

When, by the intervention of the English government, Knox was released from the French galleys in 1549, the pious young king, Edward VI, was ruling England. He was a true Protestant and his Privy Council appointed the Scottish Reformer to minister to the people and garrison of Berwick. The Anglican Church had travelled far towards a genuine Reformed Church position since the death of Henry VIII two years before, and Archbishop Cranmer had now become unequivocally Protestant in outlook. John Knox was allowed great freedom in his work at Berwick where, according to his own statement, he dispensed the Communion with the same scriptural simplicity which he had done in St Andrews. He seems to have followed in his church arrangements the example set by Calvin and Zwingli in their congregations in Switzerland. His experiences in St Andrews Castle enabled him to understand the outlook of a rough soldiery, and both his ministry to the garrison and his preaching to the citizens (among whom were many from Scotland) were successful. Here, as always, he sought to direct men to Christ as Saviour, insisting that no human priest must come between the suppliant and God. 'The rites performed by a priest save not a man.' Works of penance or of charity cannot take away sin.

While he was at Berwick, Knox made the acquaintance of Mrs Bowes, wife of Richard Bowes, the Captain of Norham Castle, six miles away. The family was of proud aristocratic lineage, and at first Richard and his brother, Sir Robert, despised Knox both because of his Protestant religion and because he had not a family descent like their own. When the Reformer fell in love with Mr and Mrs Bowes' daughter Marjory, the brothers used insulting words. He 'kept a good countenance, but the despiteful words had so pierced his heart that his life was bitter unto him'. Mrs Bowes, however, was strongly attracted to him because of the gospel message he proclaimed, and five years later he and Marjory were married.

They had a deep, mutual affection, and the encouragement and help of this gentle woman were invaluable to her husband in difficult days. She died young, leaving him with two small children, just as he was leading the Reformation movement to triumph in Scotland. Mrs Bowes had a morbid outlook, was very introspective, and was always becoming depressed by spiritual difficulties. Knox showed himself a wise and patient counsellor, and also an affectionate family man.

We must return now to the beginning of the Reformer's stay at Berwick. In 1550 he was called upon to preach before the powerful Council of the North at Newcastle and explain why he affirmed the Mass to be idolatry. Knox believed in attacking the Mass as the central doctrine of the Roman Church, and always insisted it was blatantly idolatrous. We may here notice what the Scottish Reformers meant by the term *idolatry* which they so frequently used. For them it signified 'the Mass, invocation of saints, adoration of images, and the keeping and retaining of the same; and finally, all honouring of God not contained in his holy Word'.[1] Knox was not alone in his references to this

---

1. 'The Book of Discipline' in Dunlop's *Confessions*, II, p. 523.

'idolatry'. All the Reformers maintained it was blasphemous to declare that a human being could turn the bread and wine into the very body and blood, soul and divinity of the Lord Jesus. Even the gentle Archbishop Cranmer asserted it was 'detestable idolatry', and 'manifest wickedness and idolatry'. Bishops Latimer, Hooper, Ridely and all the continental Reformers, spoke in a similar strain.

The address at Newcastle made the Council realize that Knox was no ordinary champion of Reformed doctrine. Professor Hume Brown, referring to this, writes: 'Compared with similar productions of his most distinguished English contemporaries, Cranmer, Latimer, Hooper, Knox's performance strikes us as the expression of a far more powerful nature than belonged to any of them'.[2]

In 1551, Knox was removed to Newcastle where he carried on his ministry with his usual energy, visiting many places in the North. Soon he was offered the Bishopric of Rochester. The Duke of Northumberland wanted him appointed so that he might be, he said 'as a whetstone to quicken the Archbishop of Canterbury, whereof he had need'.[3] It is suspected, however, that Northumberland wished to get him away from the North because his stern denunciations of sin troubled his conscience. The Reformer declined the bishopric, as he had previously refused the rich living of All Hallows, London, because, in his opinion, the Anglican Church had not even yet attained the scriptural purity in doctrine and Church government for which he longed.

At the end of 1551 Knox was appointed as one of the six court chaplains in spite of his withering condemnation of

---

2.   Hume Brown, *Life of John Knox*, I, pp.116, 117.

3.   J.A. Froude, *History of England*, V, p. 475.

wrongdoing in high places. He came to London, and in the autumn of 1552 took his turn in preaching before the court until the end of the year. His first sermon caused a sensation among the bishops for he 'inveighed with great freedom against kneeling at the Lord's Supper'. This question was being fiercely debated at the time in connection with the publication of Edward VI's second Prayer Book. Knox, like Bishop Hooper, John à Lasco, and many others, strongly denounced the custom of kneeling at the Communion as being recognition of the sacerdotal claim that the bread and wine were turned into the very body and blood of the Lord. Cranmer and Ridley held that kneeling was a more seemly posture and it implied no adoration of the elements. Knox, in his forthright way, argued that it was a dangerous compromise with superstition. His sermon undoubtedly had a great effect and, soon afterwards, while the kneeling posture was retained, a rubric was added in the following terms: 'For as concerning the sacramental bread and wind, they remain still in their very natural substances, and, therefore, may not be adored, for that were idolatry to be abhorred of all faithful Christians. And as concerning the natural body and blood of our Saviour Christ, they are in heaven and not here. For it is against the truth of Christ's true natural body to be in more places than in one, at one time.'[4] This addition was due to John Knox more than any other man, and represented a great triumph. High churchman have been known to describe this as the 'Black Rubric'.

There was still another triumph for Knox. Archbishop Cranmer had been engaged for four years in drawing up Articles of Religion to express the doctrinal position of the Church. There was one article dealing with ceremonies. When

---

4.   *Liturgies of Edward VI* (Parker Society), p. 283.

Knox as one of the court chaplains was consulted, he objected to this article so strongly and persistently that it was struck out. This gives us a glimpse of his driving power and of the place he had come to occupy in the Church of England. In those days the Anglican Church did not hold the doctrine of 'apostolic succession'. Preachers from the Reformed Churches were freely received, and their Orders recognized as genuine. The members of Reformed Churches from abroad were given communion without question in the Anglican Church. It was only in the days of Archbishop Laud some seventy-five years later that the Church of England began to depart from this happy position and put forward claims for 'the divine right of Episcopacy', which alienated other Reformed Churches. It is good to recall the better order of things which prevailed in the time of the great bishops of John Knox's days. It is also pleasant to remember how this unflinching Presbyterian could co-operate so closely with Anglicans and yet not bate a jot of his own testimony. At the same time his five year's association in England with the noble-hearted men who then ruled the Church must have greatly widened his sympathies.

With the untimely death of Edward VI on 6 July 1553 began one of the saddest periods in English history. In the providence of God, it was short. Mary Tudor, daughter of Henry VIII by Catherine of Aragon, ascended the throne. Like her mother she was a Roman Catholic and was, at the same time, both fanatical and morbid in outlook. She plunged the country into anguish and won for herself the terrible nature of 'Bloody Mary'. In the Parish Church of Amersham in Buckinghamshire, ten days after Edward's death, John Knox preached one of the most deeply-moving and eloquent sermons of his whole career, depicting in prophetic terms the sorrowful days about to break on England. In London he saw Mary's triumphal procession and heard the plaudits of the crowds which greeted her along the route. To some of these enthusiasts he exclaimed, in characteristic fashion, 'You are now ringing your bells, but very soon you will be wringing your hands.' He remained six months more in England, preaching in many places. Cranmer and the other evangelical bishops were, meanwhile, committed to the Tower and in a few months were burnt at the stake. In her short reign of five years Mary was responsible for condemning 286 Protestants to the same fate, and not a few died in prison because of the hard conditions.

John Knox on the Continent

The door was now closed against Knox. He could do no further work in England, and was, moreover, in constant peril. It is not surprising, therefore, that he crossed to France early in March 1554 although he had only ten groats in his pocket. Having visited several churches in Switzerland, he settled for a time in Geneva where he was attracted by John Calvin. The two Reformers had much in common. The theology of both was based firmly upon the Bible; both refused to be bound by the tradition of the Church. In this latter respect they differed somewhat from the Lutherans. It would be a mistake, however, to think that John Knox got his view of biblical truth from Calvin. He had arrived at his own conclusions independently, conclusions which were well defined when he preached his first sermon at St Andrews in 1547.

At Geneva, with England and Scotland both closed to him, Knox found a haven of refuge in a time of sore trouble. The hospitality extended so freely and generously by the church at Geneva to religious refugees from other lands reflects everlasting credit upon its members. Calvin and Knox became intimate friends. The former was approaching the zenith of his power; the latter was only beginning his work as a Protestant leader. The result of their close association was that later the Scottish Church adopted Calvin's system more wholeheartedly than any other church except, perhaps, the Reformed Church in France. Calvin was a deeply pious, reserved, and cultured French gentleman who, intellectually, stood head and shoulders above all the other churchmen of his day. Possessed in a remarkable degree of the clear logic of his race, he made the Holy Scriptures live for men as they have seldom done. His influence was felt over a very wide area, not least in Scotland, where his views and those of John Knox were eagerly absorbed.

Largely on the advice of Calvin, Knox went in November 1554 to Frankfurt as joint-pastor with Whittingham of the congregation of English exiles which had gathered there after fleeing from the persecution in England under Mary Tudor. The City Council and the Protestant community were very kind and considerate. The use of the French church was granted to the English strangers on the condition that they followed the Calvinistic forms of worship of the French Reformed Church. Problems arose over questions of ritual and the use of the service book of Edward VI. Knox repeatedly showed himself ready to assuage difficulties, and a settlement agreeable to all was reached. The peace was rudely disturbed by the arrival of Dr Cox (formerly Chancellor of Oxford University) and a fresh band of English refugees. Although received with every mark of Christian generosity, they immediately became exceedingly aggressive, insisted on a full-fledged Anglican service, and paid no attention to the contract made with the French church, or the agreement reached in the congregation itself. In a most unworthy manner they even accused Knox of treason against the Emperor, Charles I, and, as Frankfurt was an imperial city, the City Council became alarmed and prayed Knox to depart.

A large number of sympathizers followed him for four miles along the road and, with heavy hearts and many tears, bade farewell to this man who had so faithfully proclaimed to them the evangel of the grace of God.

This was a hard and bitter experience for the Reformer. By 13 September 1555 he was back in Geneva and was immediately elected as joint-pastor of the congregation of English exiles in that city. In a short time, however, he felt impelled to travel to Scotland for a brief visit, the situation being then favourable, as we have already recorded.[5] He saw that the time was not yet ripe for taking up the work in Scotland permanently, and therefore returned to his well-loved flock in Geneva early in July 1556. His sphere of labour was now eminently congenial to him, and the next two years were the happiest of his life.[6] He had in his congregation men of outstanding ability and piety. Among these was Miles Coverdale, formerly Bishop of Exeter, but now an exile for conscience's sake. He was one of Knox's best collaborators, and was very happy to discharge the duties of a Presbyterian elder in the congregation. Geneva was indeed a wonderful school for training men for the service of Christ. Knox and other British people were being unconsciously prepared to carry its spiritual dynamic to their own land. They little knew that from that beautiful city beside the mountains on the shore of Lake Leman, mighty Puritanic forces were to go forth to the ends of the earth to galvanize the religious life of many lands.

John Knox's congregation of English exiles adopted and improved the model of ecclesiastical polity set forth by Calvin in his famous *Institutes*. In Geneva he was never able to secure

5.   See chapter 5.
6.   David Laing, *The Works of John Knox*, IV, p. 240.

his own way entirely, for the civil power exercised considerable control over the church. The English congregation was free from this civil control. It has been described as 'the first Puritan congregation'. In a sense this is true, but it must not be forgotten that individuals cherishing the purest Puritannic ideals arose independently in many lands. Thus, it would not be incorrect to describe the Italian Marsilius of Padua in the 14th century, the Englishman, John Wyclif, in the same century, and the Polish nobleman, John à Lasco, in the 16th as equally 'Puritannic' in their principles. These principles consisted in taking the Bible as the inspired Word of God, treating it as the only rule of faith and morals, deliberately setting aside all appeals to tradition or to a hierarchy, and rigorously practising with great strictness the teachings of Scripture. Such men certainly did not appear for the first time in Geneva; but it was there that the first congregation of the Reformed era thoroughly embodying these principles was organized. It is also true that many of the Puritan leaders who afterwards refused to submit to Queen Elizabeth's dictatorial policy in ecclesiastical matters had been members of this remarkable congregation. Here we can find the secret of the close affinity between English Puritannism and Scottish Presbyterianism in their best days. Moreover, *The Book of Common Order*, drawn up at Geneva under Knox's guidance, was for a long time the Directory for Public Worship of the Church of Scotland, and the Geneva congregation set the example in beginning a metrical version of the Psalms. It is incorrect to suggest, as some do, that there was any essential difference between the position of John Knox and that of the earlier English Puritans.

It is worth remembering, too, that by the time he settled in Geneva, Knox had adopted those views of limited monarchy and political freedom which placed him far ahead of even

Luther and Calvin in this field. Modern democracy owes more to the teachings of the Scottish Reformer than it realizes. In this respect his views have exercised a profound effect on the whole course of Scottish Church history. As we shall see, these democratic principles appeared very clearly in his interviews with Mary of Scotland.

~~~

In 1557 Knox received an urgent call from four of the leading Scottish nobles to return home. In their view the time was now propitious for making a big Protestant advance. At great personal inconvenience and with much reluctance, he left Geneva where he had been so happy. On arrival at Dieppe on 24 October 1557 he found two letters awaiting him telling him it would be unwise to return home at that time. He was 'partly confounded, and partly pierced with anguish and sorrow'.

This disappointing experience produced two remarkable results. One was that he sent a very stern letter to his friends among the Lords in Scotland. He reminded them forcibly of their duty as magistrates or, at least, representatives of the people, and called upon them to hazard their own lives for the deliverance of their feudal subjects from the bondage which oppressed their bodies and souls. It was only for this cause, he said, that they were called 'Princes of the people'.[7] The letter had an immediate effect. On 3 December 1557 they entered into a solemn engagement called 'a Band', or 'Covenant', binding themselves to 'apply our whole power, substance, and our very lives, to maintain, set forward, and establish the most blessed Word of God and His Congregation'. This Covenant revived the drooping spirits of the leading Protestants and marked a turning-point in the story of the Reformation. For

7.   David Laing, *op. cit.*, I, p. 272.

a number of years, the term *Congregation* was used to designate the whole company of those in Scotland who sincerely accepted the Evangelical Reformation. Since, at first, the outstanding leaders of the movement were nobles, there is frequent reference to *the Lords of the Congregation*. They were soon joined by the Earl of Argyll and the Earl of Morton, men who were carefully watching the signs of the times. It was resolved that the Holy Scriptures and the Book of Common Prayer be read every Lord's Day in the churches where they had influence. The nobles were in agreement with John Knox that they should not unnecessarily provoke rebellion against the constituted authority. Hence they moved with caution and resolved that, in the meantime, doctrine, preaching and interpretation of Scripture, be 'had and used privately in quiet houses', great conventions being avoided 'till God move the Prince to grant public preaching'.[8] The citizens of the burghs of Scotland, as well as the nobles, now began to bestir themselves and to organize meetings for worship. 'Many were so strengthened, that, within a few months, we sought to have *the face of a Church* among us.'[9]

The second result of Knox's disappointment at Dieppe in 1557 was that, through his enforced residence there, he was the means, under God, of gathering and building up an immense congregation. On his first arrival in Dieppe in 1554 there were no Protestants in the town. In August 1557 a number of converts were made by French evangelists. Knox preached there that winter. A French chronicler, referring to his work in Dieppe, wrote in 1559 that 'he achieved a great result, and the number of the faithful grew in such degree that they dared

---

8. John Knox, *History*, I, pp. 136-8.
9. David Laing, *Works of Knox*, I, p. 300.

to preach in full day'.[10] A month after the departure of the Scottish preacher, between 600 and 800 took communion publicly in the Protestant fashion. In three years more, nearly all the people of Dieppe were Protestants, and the city became a foremost place in defending the Protestant cause. Nothing could show more clearly the amazing preaching power of the Scottish Reformer. Let it be remembered that his visits were short and that he was a foreigner speaking in a language other than his own. His friends put it down to the power of God; his enemies described it as something demonic.

About this time, Knox wrote some important letters and pamphlets. The first was to his *Brethren in Scotland*. It was directed against the teachings of religious fanatics like Claus Storch in Germany, and certain extremists even in Britain who held that they did not need the Ten Commandments or any moral precepts because they were led of the Spirit. The next letter was to the *Professors of the Truth in Scotland*. It discussed whether Christians, when oppressed and persecuted, were justified in rebelling. He took the view that his co-religionists should, as far as possible, be obedient to the powers that be and submit in all things not repugnant to God. They were bound, however, to defend their brethren from persecution and tyranny. It was a vital question at the time, for in England Mary Tudor was hurrying Protestants to the stake, and in Scotland the Queen Mother, Mary of Lorraine, who had been made regent in 1554, might at any moment turn on the Protestants in accordance with the persecuting policy of her Guise relatives who were ruling France. Another pamphlet embodied a *Letter to the Queen Regent with Additions*. The original letter, sent to her on the recommendation of the Earl Marischal, was exceedingly

10. Hume Brown, *Knox*, I, p. 218.

respectful and courtier-like, but it was rudely cast aside. Since then Knox had learned much as to the policy of the regent, and the *Additions* now openly justified religious revolution against a persecuting tyrant. He appealed to the Scriptures in support of his view.

Finally, he addressed a letter to *My Beloved Brethren the Commonalty of Scotland*. He gave them 'a conception of their manhood, their rights, their responsibilities, and their duties as citizens, not only of the Kingdom of Scotland but of the Kingdom of Heaven, which to them must have been a perfect revelation.'[11] Before the Reformation the governing power of Scotland was in the hands of the nobles. It was the Reformation movement which first awakened the common people to political consciousness, and this was due principally to John Knox.

All these letters embodied central points in his policy, and exercised much influence. The same cannot be said about *The First Blast of the Trumpet Against the Monstrous Regiment of Women*, written in the same period. The word 'regiment' here, of course, means 'regimen' or rule. He wrote the book at a time when he could not return to either England or Scotland because Mary Tudor was ruling in the one, and Mary of Lorraine in the other. Although the work is learned enough, its arguments against feminine rule are ill-founded, and the book should never have been written. It did incalculable harm, although the views expressed were not at all uncommon in the world at the time. Knox himself confessed to a friend afterwards that he had erred and that he regretted his 'rude vehemencie and inconsidered affirmations'. To another friend he wrote, with a touch of humour, that 'the First Blast had blown away all his friends in England'. Queen Elizabeth believed,

---

11. D. MacMillan, *John Knox*, p. 118.

when she came to the throne, that the book was written against herself and she hated John Knox to the end of his days. As a consequence, co-operation between the English and Scottish Protestants was made very difficult at a time when it was desperately called for in the interests of both.

It is most surprising that Knox, of all men, should have written such a work, for he was singularly blessed in the number and the excellence of his women friends. They were devoted to him and, in correspondence, constantly sought his advice during the whole of his ministry. His wise and tender counsel to them in times of spiritual perplexity reveals to us that he was not at all the cold, inhuman, stony-hearted man whom his enemies delight to paint for us.

The congregation at Geneva, as soon as they knew that Knox had not been able to return to Scotland, elected him forthwith as their minister once more. In March 1558 he was again at their head in the city he loved so much.

7

THE CONFLICT INTENSIFIED

With the help of her Guise counsellors, the Queen Dowager, Mary of Lorraine, succeeded in 1554 in ousting the Earl of Arran from the regency which he had occupied since 1542. He was a weak and unstable man. At first he posed as a friend of the Protestants and was hostile to Cardinal Beaton. Then, as we have seen, he made a complete *volte face*, submitted to the cardinal, did penance, dismissed his Protestant chaplains and persecuted the cause he had formerly supported. As a member of the House of Guise, the new regent could scarcely be anything else but a fanatical Roman Catholic. She and her numerous French courtiers soon turned Scotland into what was almost an appanage of France.

As her daughter, the young Queen Mary, was now of an age to marry the Dauphin, the regent very astutely sought to ingratiate herself with the Scottish Protestants so as to secure their consent to the conditions for the marriage then being arranged. Arran (now the Duke of Chatelherault) was not friendly to the regent because she had ousted him from the post. He wished, as he was next heir to the throne, to have Mary married to his own son and heir. He was encouraged in this by his brother, Archbishop John Hamilton, who had much ecclesiastical support. Hamilton leaned towards England, which was then ruled by Mary Tudor, who had made the State officially Catholic. Spain, too, was of course very friendly to Mary Tudor. The regent, therefore, needed the help of the Protestants to secure approval for the conditions proposed for the marriage of Mary to the Dauphin. It was an unusual situation. In courting the support of the Protestants, Mary of Lorraine seemed almost as if she were forgetting her family traditions. Those whom she had formerly opposed so bitterly were now received 'with benignant smiles, and dismissed with most gracious assurances'. She had a purpose to serve in courting the heretics, 'but when it was served, her countenance forthwith was changed'.[1]

The queen regent played her part with consummate success, and with the approval of the Scottish Parliament, Mary of Scotland was married to the Dauphin on 24 April 1558. With extraordinary duplicity, the French persuaded her to sign three secret treaties making over the Scottish throne to the French king in the event of her dying childless, as there was then every prospect she would because of her husband's physical condition. On 29 November 1558 the Parliament of Scotland bestowed on the Dauphin the crown matrimonial. The diplomacy of the House of Guise seemed then to be on the crest of the wave.

In the years immediately preceding these events, however, the Protestant cause in Scotland had increased greatly in strength, especially in the towns. The common people were now emerging as an important force. The opposition to the Roman Church was becoming national, and it was social as well as religious. This is shown in *The Beggar's Summonds* posted on religious houses on 1 January 1559. It professed to be from the blind, beggars, widows and other poor, and

---

1.   J. Cunningham, *Church History of Scotland*, II, p. 250.

accused the clergy of having stolen the wealth given by pious men, and warned them to remove before Whitsunday. This was undoubtedly a portent of revolutionary change.

~~~

The queen regent, having attained her diplomatic objectives, now resolved on a policy of religious repression characteristic of the House of Guise. She ordered everyone in Scotland to observe the coming Easter according to the rites of the Roman Church. She also forbade preaching by 'unauthorized persons'. The Protestants, who saw that their cause would be destroyed, sent the Earl of Glencairn and Sir Hew Campbell (Sheriff of Ayr) to make representations. The queen regent's reply was cynical: 'In despite of you and of your ministers both, they shall be banished out of Scotland albeit they preached as truly as ever did St Paul.' When reminded as to former promises to the Protestants, she made the astonishing reply: 'it became not subjects to burden their princes with promises further than it pleased them to keep the same.'[2] Knox was sadly disappointed when he heard of this for he had formerly written to John Calvin praising and commending her 'for excellent knowledge in God's Word and goodwill towards the advancement of His glory.'[3]

Mary of Lorraine now showed that she was resolutely determined to uproot completely the Protestant faith. No doubt tremendous pressure was being exercised upon her by her brothers, the Duke of Guise and the cardinal. It is more than likely, too, that the pope was egging her on. When, in the interview with Glencairn and Sir Hew Campbell already referred to, she claimed the right to break her promises, the heroic Glencairn was equal to the occasion, and said, 'Then, if

2.   John Knox, *History*, I, p. 159.

3.   John Knox, *op. cit.*, I. p. 158.

you renounce your promises, we must renounce our allegiance'. The regent was somewhat startled, but soon afterwards she summoned all the Protestant preachers in the country to appear before her on 10 May at Stirling. The large assembly of Protestants then meeting in Dundee decided to accompany them. To assure the regent that they did not come as rebels, they sent forward John Erskine of Dun, a man courteous, gentle and firm, to explain the situation. The regent became alarmed and persuaded Dun to write to his friends asking them to disperse, and promised the summonses would be withdrawn. The 10th of May arrived and the queen, forgetting her promise, commanded the preachers to be 'put to the horn'. This was a Scottish legal phrase meaning 'they would be declared rebels by the sound of the horn', and no man, under pain of high treason, could hold any communication with them.[4] It is interesting to note that Erskine of Dun, staunch Protestant though he was, always retained the deep respect of both Mary of Lorraine, and her daughter, Queen Mary of Scotland.

Hume Brown sums up the situation in Scotland in 1559 thus:

> The Catholic Church had lost hold of the mind and heart of the country, and it had now become identified with a foreign power, which had made itself odious to the bulk of the people. The policy of Mary of Lorraine now stood fully disclosed as having no other end than the subjection of Scotland to France. The people were thoroughly roused by the insolence and rapacity of the foreign soldiery ... In 1542, after the death of James V, the Catholic clergy had the heart of the country with them against England and heresy; in the growth of opinion the Protestants had become the national party and England the one hope against a foreign tyranny.[5]

---

4.   J. Cunningham, *Church History of Scotland*, I, p. 255.

5.   P. Hume Brown, *John Knox*, I, p. 346.

At this dramatic moment, when the battle was about to be joined, John Knox suddenly returned to Scotland on 2 May 1559. He had been delayed by the refusal of Queen Elizabeth to grant him permission to pass through England on his way home. He had important matters to communicate to the English government regarding affairs on the continent, and also wished to visit his old congregations at Newcastle and Berwick. The queen, however, was relentless because of her indignation against his notorious book *The First Blast of the Trumpet*, and because of his Calvinism and Puritanism. He did not receive even the courtesy of a reply. Her great minister, Sir William Cecil, himself had good grounds for being irritated with Knox, for the Reformer had formerly written to him in unmeasured terms, making wild allegations against him. To the English statesman's credit, however, he closely collaborated with Knox in the following year, and strongly impressed upon his queen the necessity of giving support to the Scottish Protestants against Mary of Lorraine and the French. He found it hard to persuade her, but finally succeeded.

After two nights in Edinburgh, where his arrival caused a sensation, Knox proceeded to Dundee where the Protestants were studying how to defend themselves against the regent's aggressive policy. When the Reformer left Scotland after his short visit in 1556 he had been burnt in effigy and declared an outlaw. The sentence was now renewed by the queen regent, and he was 'blowne loud to the horne'.[6] There is no indication that this vindictive action caused Knox any uneasiness.

---

6.   See *Wodrow Miscellany*, I, p. 57.

It is worth noting that he was accepted everywhere as unquestioned leader of the Reformation in Scotland. In 1547 he had preached for not more than a few months and only in St Andrews at that, before being carried to the French galleys. In the next twelve years he had visited his native land only once, and even then his stay was very short. He had had few opportunities, therefore, of making an impression on his countrymen. He was a man of comparatively humble origin in an age when power and influence lay in the hands of the nobles. Yet so strong was his personality that not only the commonality, but also the proudest nobles looked upon him from the start as the undoubted leader in spite of his strong democratic principles and rugged independence. It is an outstanding tribute to his undoubted greatness. We may criticize him for using rough and unguarded language in the spirit of his age, but of his greatness there can be no question. In the opinion of J.A. Froude, he was unsurpassed by any British Reformer.

He resolved to accompany his brother preachers who were summoned to appear before the regent on 10 May 1559, a few days after his return. To Mrs Locke he wrote: 'I am come, I praise my God, even in the brunt of the battle ... I intend, if God impede not, also to be present: by life, by death, or else by both, to glorify His godly name.'[7] At Perth he preached every day to a multitude of people. Excitement reached fever heat when it became known that the regent had broken her promise to Erskine of Dun, and had proclaimed the preachers outlaws. The very day that these ominous tidings reached Perth, Knox was preaching against idolatry, and no doubt the news from Stirling increased his vehemence. 'He seemed like another Demosthenes, wielding at will the mighty multitude

---

7.   David Laing, *Works of Knox*, VI, p. 21.

which had come to hear him.'[8] Most of the people had left the Church when a priest, with incredible lack of common sense, uncovered a gorgeous altar piece richly decorated with images and proceeded to celebrate Mass. When a boy protested, the priest struck him a blow on the ear. The lad retaliated by flinging a stone which broke an image. There was general uproar and the crowd surged back into the Church. Already in a state of tension because of the perfidy of the regent and her injustice to the preachers, the people were now worked up into a frenzy. 'In a few minutes every chapel was ransacked, every virgin, apostle, and saint broken to pieces.' Soon, in the street an excited mob shouted 'To the Monasteries', and in a short time the monasteries of the Black and Grey Friars, as well as the Charter House, were destroyed by what Knox called 'the rascal multitude'. Of these splendid buildings, only the walls were left standing.

These events in Perth were the signal for an outburst of fury lasting some months against many of the religious houses in different parts of the country, leading to great destruction. It has become the fashion in certain Roman Catholic and High Church circles to lay all the blame for these events upon John Knox, whom they represent as a wild and frantic iconoclast, the very embodiment of unreason and bitterness. In justice to a great man, it is worthwhile examining his relationship to the destruction which took place.

It is true he frequently thundered against 'idolatry'. But he was by no means the first to do so. In the early Church there were neither pictures nor images of sacred persons or objects. When pagans entered Christian places of worship they were perplexed

---

8.   J. Cunningham, *Church History of Scotland*, I, p. 256.

beyond measure to find no image of the deity. The Synod of Elvira in Spain in 305 protested strongly against the introduction of paintings into churches for fear they might be worshipped. At the end of the sixth century the Bishop of Marseilles was so distressed by the superstition connected with images that he ordered their destruction in his diocese. The Church in the East was convulsed by this question in the Iconoclastic Controversy during which images were completely removed; but under the influence of the empress, Irene, at the Second Council of Nicea in 787 this tendency was reversed. Images of Christ, the Virgin, angels, saints and holy men were authorized, and 'salutation and honorific worship' were to be offered them. In the West, however, no less a person than Charlemagne, with the support of the Council of Frankfurt in 794, wrote strongly against this finding in his book *Libri Carolini*.[9]

Knox and his fellow-Reformers, therefore, when they so frequently condemned *idolatry* in the Roman Church, were following in a goodly succession. It is hard to see how they could have done otherwise if they were to fulfil their mission. There is, however, no record that Knox ever incited the crowds to destroy abbeys or parish churches, as his enemies suggest. There is evidence on the contrary that more than once he tried to prevent this, as in the case of Scone Abbey where he and Lord James Stewart and the Earl of Argyll could only hold back the mob for one day. The policy of the Reformers was to leave parish churches intact after they were purged of images and other unscriptural adornments. According to Kirkcaldy of Grange, religious houses were pulled down only where the holders of them defied the new Protestant authority. This is not

9.   P. Schaff, *Medieval Christianity*, II, p. 468; S.G. Green, *Handbook of Church History*, p. 396.

so drastic as the critics tell us. The destruction of ecclesiastical buildings was common long before Knox became leader. The most beautiful Scottish abbeys had been destroyed by the English in 1523 and 1528.[10] In the 14th century a form of general excommunication had to be used in the diocese of St Andrews against 'all who burn churches or houses in time of peace.'[11] In some cases church property was destroyed by the mob in revenge for old wrongs, fancied or real. In other cases, many edifices were falling into ruin from neglect even before the Reformation. We see, then, how unfair it is for partisan writers to picture John Knox as almost the sole destroyer of ecclesiastical houses.

The most significant fact in connection with the violent outbreaks of the multitude in the destruction of the monasteries is the light they cast upon the intense feeling which prevailed at the time against the hierarchy. The pent-up indignation of past years had now broken forth in fury. The lack of confidence in the regent, who had so often broken her word, intensified the bitterness between the parties. Although she had formerly temporized very cleverly, she had recently declared vehemently her intention of driving all Protestant preachers from the land. In her rage, because of the sacking of the religious houses at Perth, she had gone to the length of declaring she would utterly destroy 'man, woman, and child in that town and consume the same by fire, and thereafter salt it, in sign of a perpetual desolation.'[12]

Naturally, such an attitude aroused intense opposition not only among the Protestant nobles but among the common

10.   See also p. 44-5

11.   David Patrick, *Statutes of the Scottish Church*, p. 75

12.   John Knox, *History*, I., p. 163.

people who were becoming a more important factor in the State. The combination against the regent was a formidable one for she had not only to contend with nobles and commoners who strongly opposed her on religious grounds, but also with many who were prepared to foment a revolution because of economic or social conditions. Besides the high-principled noblemen who supported the Reformation from conscientious motives, there were others who were casting envious eyes on the immense wealth of the Church which, they argued, had been filched from their ancestors and which they were prepared to seize by force if necessary.

The spirit of change was abroad. Feudalism was breaking up and a new merchant class was coming into prominence with more liberal ideas. Mary of Lorraine stood for the old religion, the old class privileges, and the old alliance with France which involved the presence in Scotland of much-hated foreigners. She was determined to have her way, and the many interests against her were equally resolved to secure freedom and claim their rights. Matters had reached an *impasse*, and both sides prepared to appeal to the arbitrament of the sword.

8

THE STRUGGLE CONTINUES

We have seen how the regent at Stirling had threatened to banish every Protestant preacher from the realm, and had declared that she would raze Perth to the ground. John Knox in his *History* relates how he and his friends

> 'suspecting nothing such cruelty, but thinking that such words might escape her in choler, without purpose determinate, because she was a woman set afire by the complaints of those hypocrites who flocked unto her, as ravens to a carrion; We (we say) suspecting nothing such beastly cruelty, returned to our own houses ...
>
> 'But she, set afire, partly by her own malice, partly by commandment of her friends in France, and not a little by bribes, which she and Monsieur d'Oysel received from the bishops and the priests here at home, did continue in her rage.'[1]

Continuing his narrative, Knox tells how the regent 'sent for all the nobility, to whom she complained that we meant nothing but rebellion ... and by such other persuasions she made the most part of them grant to pursue us. And then incontinent sent she for her Frenchmen; for that was and hath ever been her joy to see Scottishmen dip one with another's blood.'[2]

---

1.   John Knox, *History*, I. p. 163.
2.   *Op. cit.*, I, pp. 163, 164.

Knox did not lay all the blame on the queen regent, for, after mentioning the Duke of Chatelherault, 'led by the cruel beast, the Bishop of St Andrews, and by those that yet abuse him', he went on, 'These and such other pestilent Papists ceased not to cast faggots on the fire, continually crying, "Forward upon these heretics; we shall once rid this realm of them".[3]

The Protestant leaders, hearing of the intention of the regent to attack the Congregation, met in the town of Perth and despatched to her a very respectful letter expressing their loyalty to the Authority of Scotland, and to her Grace, but at the same time declaring 'with most dolorous minds' that they were constrained 'by unjust tyranny purposed against them' to declare to her Grace 'that except this cruelty be stayed by your wisdom, we will be compelled to take the sword of just defence against all that shall pursue us for the matter of religion, and for our conscience sake; which ought not, nor may not be subject to mortal creatures, further than by God's word man be able to prove that he hath power to command us.'[4] Similar letters were sent to the French leaders in Scotland urging them not to fight against the people of the country. At the same time stern and earnest communications were addressed to the nobles who were hostile to the Reformed cause, and to 'the Generation of Antichrist, the Pestilent Prelates and their Shavelings within Scotland' urging them to desist from war and seek the ways of peace and warning them that, otherwise, they would be met with the strongest resistance. 'Be ye assured', declared the Congregation, 'that with the same measure that ye have measured against us, and yet intend to measure to others, it shall be measured unto you.'[5]

---

3.   John Knox, *History*, I, p. 164.

4.   *Op. cit.*, I, p. 164.

5.   *Op. cit.*, I, p. 72.

All remonstrance, however, was in vain, for the regent, knowing that the military forces at the disposal of the Protestants in Perth were weak, advanced on the town with 8,000 men under d'Oysel, the French military representative. She had failed to reckon with the ability and enthusiasm of Alexander, the Earl of Glencairn, who, learning of the peril of his co-religionists, hastily assembled an army of 2,500 men in Ayrshire and with some other barons from the west arrived at Perth by forced marches through the hills. They were in time to join with the forces which had come from Fife, Angus, the Mearns and the town of Dundee, to resist unjust aggression. The brilliant action of Glencairn in bringing his men along little known mountain paths to Perth in record time took the regent and her forces completely by surprise. So alarmed were they that they entered immediately into negotiations with the Protestants to come to a pacific arrangement. The latter, anxious to show that they were not actuated by motives of rebellion, agreed to a treaty that both armies should be disbanded, that the town of Perth be left open to the queen regent, that no one should be persecuted for any of the events in connection with the recent change of religion, that the regent would allow the Reformed faith to go forward, and that at her departure she would leave the town free from French soldiers.[6]

The regent, however, had scarcely entered Perth when she shamefully broke her pledges once more. So Argyll, Lord James Stewart (her stepson), Lord Ruthven, the Earl of Menteith, and Sir William Murray of Tullibardine, all forsook her standard because of her duplicity, and went over to the opposite party. This was a matter of great importance to the Protestants. Lord James Stewart, in particular, was to

---

6.   John Knox, *History*, I. p. 176.

prove a tower of strength to the Reformed cause, for after John Knox, he became its leading spirit.

On 30 May 1559 after they had entered into a solemn covenant to defend their faith and stand by one another, the leaders of the Congregation, with a large body of men, set out for St Andrews. The first reference to the *Congregation* was in the 'band' or covenant drawn up by some lords on 3 December 1557.[7] The term embraced all those in the realm who truly accepted the Reformed religion, but we hear most frequently of the 'Lords of the Congregation', the nobles who accepted the evangelical faith. At first the aim was chiefly religious, to arrange for the printing and preaching of the gospel, the formation of local groups or congregations, the promotion of sound morality, and the administration of the sacraments. By the end of 1558 the various groups were given 'the face of a Church' by the creation of an authority to exercise discipline. Elders were appointed and godly laymen were recognized as preachers of the Word to make up for the lack of ordained ministers. In May 1559 we see the Congregation as a still more highly organized entity. The necessity of self defence had compelled them to gather together an army. They are now not only a religious body but a strong political force with their own Secretary and many recognized leaders, ecclesiastical, civil and military.

In the early days of June, on the way to St Andrews with the leaders of the movement, John Knox preached at Cupar and the neighbouring towns of Crail and Anstruther. At this time he recalled a remarkable experience which he had had twelve years before as he toiled as a slave in a French galley.

7.   Cf. p. 78.

One afternoon he had seen in the distance the towers of St Andrews across the waters. At that moment he felt that God was giving him an assurance that he would, yet again, proclaim the evangel in that loved city. He now resolved to preach in the cathedral there on 11 June 1559 in full confidence that the Lord would be with him. Archbishop Hamilton, knowing the power of the Reformer's eloquence, was aghast at the prospect. He hurried from Falkland, twenty miles away, with 300 armed men, and boasted that most of the cannon balls would alight on the Reformer's nose. Knox's friends earnestly besought him to abandon his design, but their counsels were wasted on the fearless preacher. Next morning the Archbishop, in spite of his military aid, became alarmed, and beat a hasty retreat to Falkland where the queen regent was in residence.

Knox preached in the Cathedral to a vast congregation which included many of the learned doctors of the university. His theme was 'The Ejection of the Buyers and Sellers from the Temple'. And his words proved specially moving, perhaps because of the emotional impulse from old memories. The Provost and Magistrates of the city resolved 'to remove all monuments of idolatry'.[8] A week previously there was no enthusiasm in St Andrews for the Reformation, but when Knox had preached for four days, the majority of the citizens came over to his side. Later on, a large number of the Roman Catholic clergy in the city joined the Protestant movement.

At Cupar Muir the armies of the regent and of the Congregation confronted one another. It seemed as if, suddenly, men 'rained from the clouds' to defend the Protestant cause. The regent, taken aback, asked for an eight-day truce, promising to send commissioners to arrange conditions. They never arrived.

8.   John Knox, *History*, I., pp. 181-3.

She was merely gaining time to secure more reinforcements from France. The Lords of the Congregation then attacked the garrison at Perth and compelled a surrender.

About this time Knox made formal proposals for soliciting aid from England. He and Sir William Kirkcaldy of Grange had previously discussed the matter privately. These two men, so different in many ways, had this in common, that neither expected any material gain from the Reformation. They contended for it for one reason only: they believed it was good. Knox was cosmopolitan because of his residence abroad, and knew that the Protestant cause in Scotland could scarcely survive without an alliance with England. Kirkcaldy, as a good soldier, knew that the almost untrained militia of the nobles could not beat the well-equipped, veteran soldiers of France. At this time, the Scottish troops almost regarded soldiering as an odd job to be engaged in only when agricultural pursuits made it convenient. When there was no actual fighting they were apt to disperse and go home. The laird of Grange saw that this was hopeless. On these grounds, he, too, wanted an alliance with England. Although Kirkcaldy died at last as a supporter of Queen Mary, he and Knox regarded one another with respect to the end.

At first John Knox, as Secretary to the Congregation, carried on the correspondence with the English government. He was glad to be replaced by Maitland of Lethington, a brilliant diplomat, but a somewhat supple politician. His finesse in dealing with Queen Elizabeth, who contracted a liking for him, was very different from the blunt, direct, and unflinching methods of Knox who never flattered the great ones of the earth. A man like Knox was required to deal with the shams and subterfuges of political life; and while they were often exasperated by his methods, the members of the English Council knew he was inflexibly honest. It may well be argued that in the work of bringing England and Scotland together, he did more even than the courtly Lethington who lacked the Reformer's strong moral fibre.

At this time the regent and her advisers did much mischief by circulating evil reports as to the aims of the Congregation. Its leaders were branded as fanatical revolutionaries with no religious principle. Knox's pointed manifestos were of immense value in counteracting this propaganda. His labours as a preacher were indefatigable as he travelled from place to place, and this also was of priceless help.

JJC

The Congregation, cheered by the successes at Perth and Stirling, returned to Edinburgh. The regent prudently retreated to Dunbar. Her propaganda, especially against Lord James, caused suspicions among the Protestants and many withdrew. Mary, knowing this, then marched on Edinburgh. A humiliating truce was accepted by the Congregation on 24 July 1559. They were to evacuate the capital, submit to the king, queen and regent, and refrain from molesting ecclesiastics. The other side promised that the people of Edinburgh could freely choose their religion and that Protestant preachers would have full liberty of speech. The Congregation moved to Stirling.

Meanwhile Mary of Scotland had become Queen of France on the accession of her husband to the throne, as Francis II. They immediately sent out threatening letters to her half-brother, Lord James, to which he replied with dignity saying he had done nothing against God and their majesties, and that he wanted only a reformation of the Church. Large numbers of French troops were despatched to Scotland, and the regent strengthened the fortifications at Leith. There also arrived a legate from the pope, and three learned doctors from the Sorbonne, to help cleanse Scotland from 'heretical pravity'.

The Congregation intensified their efforts to reach an agreement with the English government. Throckmorton, the English ambassador in Paris, who knew the dangers of the time in Europe, was earnestly urging upon his government the need for immediate action and collaboration with John Knox whose worth, at such a time, he knew. The stumbling-block was Queen Elizabeth who not only hated Knox but disliked the thorough-going Protestantism which was growing up in Scotland. Her personal choice would have been a Church with herself as supreme governor, but chiefly Roman Catholic in doctrine and forms of worship. She made the excuse that England and France were at peace and that she could not help *de jure* rebels in Scotland. She was finally persuaded that if the French prevailed in Scotland they would topple her from her own throne. It was this argument, dexterously used by Lethington, not the question of religion, which led Elizabeth at last to aid the Scottish Protestants.

At this time, the Earl of Arran returned from the continent. Unlike his father, the Duke of Chatelherault, he was a staunch Protestant. Being next in succession to the throne after his father, hope was widely cherished that he might marry Queen Elizabeth. His presence greatly animated the Congregation, and his weak father became Protestant once again. The Congregation felt the time for action had come, and advanced on Edinburgh which they entered on 18 October 1559. They sent a demand to the regent that all Frenchmen be asked to leave. The request was indignantly refused. On 21 October the Protestant nobles, as born counsellors of the realm, formally deposed Mary of Lorraine from the regency, ostensibly not on religious grounds, but because of her unconstitutional government and the intolerable tyranny of the French.

The difficult task of besieging the strong fortifications of Leith was begun. An attempt to scale the walls proved a costly and utter failure because of the skill of the French troops and the fewness of the Protestant soldiers. Some Protestant Scots were holding back because the suggestion of the alliance with England seemed to them perilous. The English, they feared, might replace the French as oppressors. The Roman Catholic Scots were, naturally, on the other side. In various sorties and skirmishes, the French were successful. One day they reached the Canongate of Edinburgh, inflicting considerable damage, killing civilians, and shattering the Protestant morale. A feeling of despair seized upon many. Knox records ' ... the courage of many was dejected. With great difficulty could men be retained in the town; yea, some of the greatest determined with themselves to leave the enterprise.'[9] One of the few who never lost heart was Knox himself. He preached daily to large congregations in St Giles, and his powerful eloquence and strong faith helped to arouse the enthusiasm of his hearers. Indeed, it was only his influence and optimism that kept the party from a complete break up.

On 6 November the French issued forth in considerable strength from Leith. Notwithstanding dejection and divided counsels, the Earl of Arran, Lord James and Kirkcaldy of Grange, sallied out of Edinburgh with their men and heroically drove the French towards Restalrig. They were placed in danger, however, because of the marshes in that quarter, and, finally, they suffered very heavy losses between the Calton Hill and Salisbury Crags. They narrowly escaped complete destruction.

9.   John Knox, *History*, I, p. 261.

Edinburgh Castle was in the hands of Lord Erskine, but he would give satisfaction to neither party. At midnight the Congregation fled to Stirling. It was their darkest hour. Knox relates how, in the time of trial, the ribald mob which two days previously had fawned upon them, now railed upon them, calling them traitors and heretics.[10]

Before leaving Edinburgh, Knox had preached on Psalm 80:1-3. Soon after reaching Stirling he continued his discourse, speaking from verses 4-8 of the same Psalm. It was a sermon for that dismal day. Its effect was notable and was spoken of for long afterwards.[11] Knox assured his depressed audience that, although they were being punished for former sins, if they turned sincerely to God their sorrow would be changed into joy, and their fear to boldness. Whatever became of them and their carcases, the cause of God would finally prevail in Scotland. Under the burning words of the preacher each man became heroic. Of a similar sermon, Randolph, the English ambassador, wrote to Cecil: 'The voice of one man is able in one hour to put more life in us than five hundred trumpets continually blustering in our ears.' Although darker times were still to come, the sermon at Stirling was a turning-point in the history of the Reformation.

From Stirling, one section of the Lords went to St Andrews with Knox, the other to Glasgow to protect the Protestant work in the West. About Christmas 1559, d'Oysel with 2,500 Frenchmen captured Stirling. Then he passed into Fife in an advance towards St Andrews. Reinforcements kept reaching him by sea. His advance in Fife caused the Congregation much anxiety. In this dangerous situation certain Protestant leaders

10.   John Knox, *op. cit.*, I, pp. 262-5.

11.   See Aikman's *Buchanan*, II, p. 422; *Wodrow Miscellany*, I. p. 72.

wrought prodigies of valour. Knox paid a great tribute to the Earl of Arran and Lord James. 'The said Earl, and Lord James did as they were appointed, albeit their company was very small; and yet they did so valiantly, that it passed all credibility: for twenty and one days they lay in their clothes; their boots never came off; they had skirmishing every day; yea, some days, from morn to even.'[12] The French had 4,000 soldiers, the Lords never more than 500 horsemen and 100 infantry. When reduced to only 200 they declared they would resist even with twenty men. At Burntisland, Kinghorn and Dysart there was much skirmishing and destruction of property. It was a serious time. On 31 December, Knox declared that one day of that trouble had more pierced his heart than all his sufferings in the French galleys.

Three weeks later, however, succour unexpectedly appeared. The French were only six miles from St Andrews and were flushed with success. Seeing a fleet of armed vessels entering the Forth, they concluded it must be the Marquis d'Elboeuf, brother of the Duke of Guise, with a strong force from France which would crush the Protestants once for all. Thinking their worries were at an end, they fired a salute of welcome. What was their chagrin, however, to discover that it was an English fleet, under Admiral Winter, come to block the Firth of Forth against the landing of fresh French troops. Two supply ships were seized before the very eyes of d'Oysel, and smaller ones driven aground and destroyed. When the larger English vessels appeared, consternation filled the French. 'They tore their beards and used bad language,' and immediately began a hasty retreat towards Stirling. 'They retired more in one day than they had advanced in ten.' Pursued by the infuriated populace, they found no rest until they entered the fort at Leith.

---

12. John Knox, *History*, I, pp. 278, 279.

On 27 January 1560 an agreement for mutual defence was signed at Berwick by English and Scottish representatives. This implied sending an English army into Scotland. Out of deference to Elizabeth, the religious question was not stressed. On 4 April 1560, an army of 9,000 Englishmen and 10,000 Scots joined together at Prestonpans and fraternized in amity after centuries of conflict. Common aims united them. It had been very difficult, however, to overcome old suspicions. Some still dreaded that Queen Elizabeth had sinister aims in sending her army into Scotland.

The allied siege of Leith began on 6 April 1560. Lord Grey the English commander soon discovered that Queen Elizabeth and Cecil need not have been so critical of the small success of the Congregation in attacking this fortress. It was a most difficult task. There were costly skirmishes. On 14 April the French broke through the allied trenches, killing over 200 men; and in a combined attack on the fortress on 7 May the English and Scots were severely repulsed losing 800 dead and wounded. By the end of May only 5,000 were carrying on the siege. The Lords of the Congregation became troubled. There were suspicious comings and goings which caused uneasiness. At the request of the regent, Sir James Crofts and Sir George Howard, English representatives, interviewed her. It turned out that Crofts was an enemy of the Congregation, and was secretly endeavouring to injure them with his government.[13] Underground forces were trying to break the alliance with England. Monluc, the Bishop of Valence, a most experienced diplomat, appeared in the English camp. At the same time he tried to bring about a reconciliation between the Congregation and the

13. See *Wodrow Miscellany*, I., pp. 82, 83.

regent. His movements were in danger of arousing suspicion and division among the Protestants. To prevent this the leaders drew up a new Covenant to set forward the Reformation, and in which they agreed to have no dealings with enemies without the knowledge of the Council. The Earl of Morton and the Earl of Huntly signed the document and definitely joined the Congregation — a clear indication which way the tide of success was flowing, for they were ever careful of their own interests. Other waverers followed their example and joined the Protestants.

Meanwhile, every party to the conflict was becoming weary of the strife. In France, the Guises had serious trouble with the Huguenots and could send no more soldiers to Scotland. Their fleet, under d'Elboeuf, had been badly shattered by a tempest on the way to the Forth and had to return to Dieppe. Queen Elizabeth, never very enthusiastic about the enterprise, grudged the heavy loss of men and money; whilst the Lords of the Congregation longed for an end to the strife, fearing that a prolongation of the fight might lead to an unsatisfactory settlement.

Negotiations for peace were hastened by the death of the queen regent on 10 June 1560. Realizing that death was approaching, she had sought entrance into Edinburgh Castle which, under the command of Lord Erskine, was vaguely neutral ground. To the end, however, she watched public affairs very closely and rejoiced when her cause was triumphing. Thus, when the French won a victory at Kinghorn on 7 January, she had burst forth, 'Where is now John Knox's God? My God is now stronger than his, yea, even in Fife'.[14] Before she died, however, she expressed a desire to confer with the Protestant lords. Chaterlherault, the Earls of Argyll, Marischal and Glencairn, with her step-son

---

14.   John Knox, *History*, I, p. 277.

Lord James, visited her. She lamented the troubles of Scotland and her own part in compelling them to appeal to England, and acknowledged she had been misled by unwise advisers. She urged them to send both French and English out of the country, but to maintain an alliance with France of which Mary of Scotland was queen. Finally, bursting into tears, she asked pardon from all she had offended, and declared that with all her heart she forgave all who offended her. Then she kissed them one by one. They were deeply stirred and suggested that John Willock should minister to her on her deathbed. She agreed, and 'talked with him a reasonable space'. He 'did plainly show unto her the virtue and strength of the death of Christ'. He also referred to the vanity of the Mass. 'She did openly confess that there was no salvation but in and by the death of Christ'. Knox declares it was 'a great victory for Christ'.[15]

It is a moving story. Hers had been a difficult and trying part to play in life. Her offences against the Protestants were largely the outcome of her extraordinary deference to her cruel and fanatical Guise brothers who virtually ruled France. She was deeply devoted to the Roman Church, although there were times when she seemed almost inclined to favour toleration. She could be kind and warm-hearted. Her faults were grave, but owed much to the wicked and tyrannical atmosphere in which she was reared.

On 16 June 1560 commissioners from England and France met to conclude peace. After difficult negotiations the Treaty of Edinburgh was signed on July 6th. The French and English were to leave Scotland; the fortifications of Leith (which had

15.   John Knox, *op. cit.*, I, p. 322.

never been breached) were to be destroyed; and Parliament was to be summoned for 10 July and was to be as valid as if summoned by the queen and her husband. It was known that the religious question could be raised in Parliament, for the Congregation were now virtually masters of the country. The chief credit for this happy ending of the stern struggle was due, first and foremost, to John Knox, Lord James Stewart, John Erskine, Laird of Dun, and the Earl of Glencairn. Others made a notable contribution, but these were the heroic men who, because of deep religious conviction, could be relied on to stand by the cause in fair weather and foul.

One of the most notable results of the Reformation struggle was the drawing closer together of Scotland and England in defence of common aims. For the first time in history, English troops were loudly cheered as they marched through the streets of Edinburgh prior to their departure for home

9

Victory At Last

The Treaty of Edinburgh, under which the French and English troops were removed from Scotland, had laid down that a Parliament should be called for 10 July 1560, and that a Commission for it should be sent from the king and queen in France. This Convention was to be as lawful in every way as if it had been arranged for at the express command of their Majesties. It duly met on the specified date, and was adjourned until 1 August to give time for adequate preparations. Competent authorities have described this meeting of the Three Estates as the most important ever held in Scotland. Before this great Convention assembled, a special service of thanksgiving was held in St Giles' Church attended by the nobility and a vast number of the Protestant community. After a sermon preached by John Knox 'public thanks were given unto God for His merciful deliverance,' and one petition referred to 'our confederates of England, the instruments by whom we are now set at this liberty.'[1]

The importance of this Parliament is shown by the fact that never before had so many members attended. According to the old laws of Scotland, not only the nobility but also the great land-owners who held their charters directly from the crown

---

1.　John Knox, *History*, I., p. 333.

had the privilege of membership. Owing to the expense and the difficulties of travel many of the latter class had not attended for a long time. Over a hundred of them now claimed their seats, although they had never been in Parliament before. The burghs were also well represented.

For a week a discussion went on as to whether Parliament could meet, considering that no commission had yet been received from the queen. It was decided that under the Treaty of Edinburgh they were warranted in doing so. William Maitland of Lethington was the elected Speaker. The real business of the session began on 8 August when the members of the Estates went in procession from Holyrood Palace up the steep ascent of the royal mile to the Tolbooth which was then the Parliament house. It was immediately to the west of St Giles', where the location is still marked by brass tablets in the pavement. Immediately after the session was constituted, a petition was presented from certain Protestant barons, gentlemen, burgesses and others, calling upon the house to 'redress such enormities as manifestly are, and of long time have been committed by the placeholders of the ministry, and others of the clergy, within this realm.' They asked that the 'many pestiferous errors' of the Roman Church should be disavowed, that the purity of worship and the primitive discipline of the Church be restored, and that the ample ecclesiastical revenues be applied to three noble ends, viz. the support of a gospel ministry, the promotion of education and the care of the poor. When the document had been read, the petitioners were called, and the ministers were instructed to draw up in plain and several heads the sum of that doctrine which they would maintain and desire the Parliament to establish.[2]

2.   John Knox, *op. cit.*, 1, pp. 335-8.

This work of drawing up a Confession of Faith was entrusted to six of the Scottish reformers: Knox, Spottiswood, Willock, Row, Douglas and Winram who, by a remarkable coincidence, each bore the Christian name of John. In the incredibly short space of four days they presented their Confession. It is true that as far back as April, they may have received hints as to the desirability of preparing it, but even so, its production in so short a time was remarkable. Obviously it was largely the work of John Knox. On the continent he had been familiar with several of the Protestant Confessions which had been drawn up there, and this, no doubt, helped the Scottish Reformers. Nevertheless, while the Scots Confession agreed generally with the other Creeds of the Reformed Churches, it had its own special characteristics.

Although the Archbishop of St Andrews (Primate), with the Bishops of Dunkeld and Dunblane, together with some of the inferior clergy of the Roman Church were present representing the Spiritual Estate, Parliament adopted the Confession with great enthusiasm. One of the most extraordinary things about the Scottish Reformation is the feebleness of the opposition of the Roman Catholic bishops to the various steps by which their Church was overthrown. This occasion was no exception. The points raised by the bishops were so trivial and inept, that it was considered they 'spake nothing' against the Acts being passed. This defection of the bishops and their failure to defend their Church is not easy to explain. When, for example, they were commanded by the pope to attend the Council of Trent, they unanimously refused. That able and accurate Roman Catholic historian, Father J.H. Pollen, S.J., records his opinion that 'No index can better point to the weak spot in the old Scottish Church than this faint-hearted answer of the episcopate to the summons to Trent'.[3] Henry Sinclair, Bishop of Ross, who, by this

---

3.   J.H. Pollen, *Counter Reformation*, pp. 20, 21.

time, was President of the Court of Session, churlishly replied to De Gouda, the nuncio who presented the pope's summons, that he was 'positively vexed at being asked,' and added 'I do not thank you at all'.[4] Dr Donald Maclean comments: 'In view of the wholesale defection of the higher clergy, it is not surprising that throughout the length and breadth of Scotland the lower clergy disappeared from view almost as swiftly as hoar frost before the rising sun.'

Of the Temporal Estate, five voted against the Confession of Faith which meant the setting up of the new religion. But the only argument they could bring forward was 'we will believe as our fathers believed'. In coming to a decision, each member of the House was called upon, in turn, to express his opinion individually. Many of them did so in deeply affecting terms. Randolph, the English Ambassador, who was present, described the dramatic scene to Cecil. He tells how, when the articles were approved one by one, some of the nobles were so moved that they started forward, 'offering to shed their blood in defence of the same'. The aged Lord Lindsay, 'as grave and goodly a man as ever I saw', expressed his attitude in these words: 'I have lived many years; I am the oldest in this company of my sort; now that it hath pleased God to let me see this day, where so many nobles and others have allowed so worthy a work, I will say, with Simeon, *Nunc dimittis*'.[5] 'I never heard,' says the English envoy in the same communication, 'matters of so great importance, neither sooner despatched nor with better will agreed unto.' He further declared that the Lords gave their consent with 'as glad a will as ever I heard men speak ... Divers with protestation of their conscience and faith, desired rather

---

4.   J.H. Pollen, *Papal Negotiations*, p. 134.

5.   Despatch from Randolph to Cecil, 19 August 1560 (State Papers).

presently to end their lives than ever to think contrary to that allowed there.' One of the most striking declarations was made by William Keith, the fourth Earl Marischal, known as a wise counsellor: 'It is long since I have had some favour unto the truth, and since that I have had a suspicion of the Papistical religion; but, I praise my God, this day has fully resolved me in the one and the other. For seeing that my Lords Bishops who, for their learning can, and for the zeal that they should bear to the verity would, as I suppose, gainsay anything that directly repugns to the verity of God; seeing, I say, my Lords Bishops here present speak nothing in the contrary of the doctrine proponed, I cannot but hold it to be the very truth of God, and the contrary to be deceivable doctrine. And, therefore, so far as lieth in me, I approve the one and damn the other.'[6] In this connection it should be remembered that there were also present outstanding Church leaders who had become Protestant, such as the Bishop of Galloway, various abbots, and a number of other ecclesiastical dignitaries.

The acceptance by Parliament of the Confession of Faith on 17 August 1560 marked the beginning of a new era in the history of the country. The Creed therein enshrined was taken as expressing the religion of the Scottish people, and Roman Catholic dogmas, in so far as they departed from Scripture truth, were emphatically rejected. Some have described this date as 'the birthday of a people'. The statement is true in the sense that from then onwards the common man, the artisan and the peasant, felt himself called upon to deal with sacred things in an individual and personal way such as had seldom been known anywhere since the early centuries of Christianity.

6.   John Knox, *History*, I., p 339. See also Randolph's version in *Calendar of Scottish Papers*, I, No. 886.

The Lord Jesus was now known to be the only Mediator between God and man. He was the great High Priest. Every believer had now himself become a priest unto God and had the privilege of coming direct to the throne of grace. The effect on Christian character was immense. In the words of Thomas Carlyle, 'Common man, as he was, the vague, shoreless universe had become for him a firm city, and a dwelling place which he knew.' His mind reached up to the Eternal as never before, and he realized, as his fathers had not done, how he, a mortal, sinful man, could become an heir of God through the free grace of the Redeemer. He became conscious that, while he was a citizen of Scotland, he was also a citizen of the kingdom of Christ in Scotland. He was not only a subject of the Scottish sovereign, but, above all, a subject of the King who is invisible. This made him morally strong and independent, ready to contend for truth and righteousness no matter what the great ones of the earth might say. We have here an explanation of much in the subsequent history of Scotland.

Of the great event of 17 August 1560, Dr Thomas McCrie writes:

In Scotland, the people were converted to the Protestant faith, before the civil power had moved a step in the cause: and when the Legislature became friendly to the Reformation, nothing remained for it to do, but to ratify the profession which the nation had adopted ... The nation, by its rulers and representatives, passed from Popery to Protestantism; and in its civil capacity, ratified (not the gospel indeed, which no acts of Parliament can ratify) but the profession of the gospel, which the people, in their religious capacities, had already embraced. And thus it appears that there was a civil establishment of the true religion in Scotland, before there was even an Established Church, for the Reformed Church of Scotland was not as yet regularly organized, much less endowed. The legal recognition of the Presbyterian Church, as an organized society, was a subsequent step, and indeed not fully obtained for many years after this; the settlement of regular stipends on the ministers was later still.[7]

To finish their work in regard to religion, the Parliament on 24 August 1560 passed three more Acts:

1. *An Act repealing all former Acts of Parliament contrary to the Word of God and the Confession of Faith recently adopted.* This decreed that all previous statutes regarding the censures of the Church or the worshipping of saints should be annulled.

2. *An Act for abolishing of the pope and his usurped authority in Scotland.*[8] The pope was to have no jurisdiction nor authority within the realm in time coming.

3. *An Act against the Mass and the sayers and hearers thereof.* This Act laid down that as the Roman Church has corrupted the Sacraments of Baptism and the Lord's Supper, no person shall administer the sacraments unless he is admitted and has power to that effect; nor say Mass, nor hear Mass, nor be present under the pain of confiscation of goods for the first offence, banishment for the second and death for the third.

On the face of it, this enactment looks extremely intolerant, and is certainly contrary to the practice of Protestant countries in the nineteenth, twentieth and twenty-first centuries. It has usually been urged in extenuation that the principles of religious liberty

---

7.   T. McCrie, *Sketches of Scottish Church History* (1841), pp. 65, 66.

8.   *Acts Parl. Scot.*, II, 534, c.2.

were not then so fully understood and that our ancestors still carried with them some of the intolerance of the Roman Church from which they had escaped. The correct interpretation of this severe statute, however, seems to be that it was never intended to be executed in its full extent unless in some case of extreme danger to Church and State. Eustace Percy is correct when he writes: 'Such penalties were common form in the Scottish legislation of the day; death, for instance, was the punishment prescribed by an Act of 1551 for ferrymen on the Forth overcharging their passengers. They were the lawyers' version of popular hyperbole, threats half meant and never executed.'[9] In the fifteenth century, there were laws against shooting at deer, wild beasts or wild fowl under pain of death.[10] The statute regarding the Mass became law in the period of the Council of Trent when the Counter Reformation was being launched under the lead of the Jesuits. Their record for intrigue, and even massacre, will explain why the Scots wanted to have on the statute book a severe law to be put in operation only in the case of dire extremity. In spite of all that has been written to the contrary, the Reformation in Scotland was carried out in a remarkably peaceful, thorough, and bloodless manner. No less fervent a Roman Catholic than John Lesley (1527-96), Bishop of Ross, an ardent supporter of Queen Mary, wrote: 'Yet the clemency of the heretic nobles must not be left unmentioned, since at that time they exiled few Catholics on the score of religion, imprisoned fewer, and put none to death.'[11] It was with genuine pride that Dr Thomas McCrie could write in his *Sketches of Scottish Church History* that 'not a single Papist suffered death in Scotland for the sake of his religion.'

---

9.   Eustace Percy, *John Knox*, p. 341.

10.   D. Hay Fleming, *Mary Queen of Scots*, p. 283.

11.   Quoted by D. Hay Fleming, *Reformation*, p. 437.

Sir James Sandilands, Lord of St John, was despatched to Queen Mary in Paris to secure her signature to the Act approving the Confession of Faith and the other Acts bearing upon the change of Religion in Scotland. Although these enactments had been passed almost unanimously by the Three Estates of Parliament, her Majesty expressed her displeasure with what had happened in her Scottish kingdom. John Knox's comment was, 'But how the said Lord of Saint John was entreated we list not rehearse, but always no ratification brought he unto us. But that we little regarded, or yet do regard; for all that we did was rather to show our dutiful obedience than to beg of them any strength to our religion which from God has full power, and needeth not the suffrage of man.'[12] This is undoubtedly true, for the Reformation in Scotland was brought about contrary to the will of the Sovereign. Although Mary and her husband, Francis, refused to subscribe these statutes, they were put in force, and even the Queen herself on her return to Scotland in 1561 promised not to upset the religious settlement approved by Parliament.[13]

---

12.   John Knox, *History*, I., p. 342.

13.   Cf. pp. 149, 150-1, 190-1.

10

The Principles of the Scottish Reformation

As the name indicates, the Reformation was a forming again of the Church founded by Christ and the apostles. Basically it was simply a going back to the truths and ideals of the early Christian Church. The Church of the apostles provides for all time a model as to creed and conduct. In the Old Testament we see how God enjoined Moses as regards the tabernacle, 'See that thou make all things according to the pattern showed to thee in the mount' (Exod. 25:40; Heb. 8:5). The Reformers took the view that, in the same way, the Church set up by our Lord and His apostles has been given as a pattern for all ages.

In the course of time, the Church departed step by step from this early model, in both doctrine and practice, until it had become almost unrecognizable as the same Church. The result of this playing fast and loose with the teachings and example of Christ and His apostles was sad deterioration and corruption. Hence the need for a strong reforming movement to return to the simplicity and purity of the early Church. The Reformers attained this great end by adhering faithfully to certain leading principles.

1. They returned to the Bible as the supreme rule of faith and morals.

All the Reformers believed that, in order to bring new life to the Church and really to know God's will, they must get back to the

Holy Scriptures given by God Himself through divine revelation. Like the men of the Westminster Abbey, eighty-three years later, they held that the Word of God, which is contained in the Old and New Testaments, is the only rule to direct us in the matter of our salvation and our duty to God, and that, indeed, it teaches us all what we are to believe concerning God. Here they found the guide for men in all matters of faith and for every situation in life.

The Roman Church forbade the laity to read the Bible in the vernacular. When it was read in Church, it was read in Latin, a language which very few people could understand. The Reformers wrought a mighty change in this respect. They put the Word of God into the hands of all kinds of people, and it proved indeed to be the 'word of life', bringing to men of all classes a personal knowledge of the love of God in Christ Jesus for perishing men. The Scriptures led them direct to the fountain of living waters. They were no longer dependent on a fallible and often extremely ignorant priesthood.

It is true that the Roman Church accepted the Bible as the inspired Word of God, but she did not give it to the people. She also accepted the Apocryphal Books of the Old Testament which contain much legend and other unreliable matter and so are liable to foster error. Moreover, the Roman Church took the Latin Vulgate translation made by Jerome early in the fifth century as the only authoritative version of the Scriptures in the Church of Rome. While it is a very wonderful translation and commands our admiration as the product of one man's labours, nevertheless it contains certain serious errors in rendering the original languages. For example, the injunction 'Repent' is rendered 'Do penance', and a number of similar errors help to bolster up the Roman Church system.

Even more serious is the place given by the Church of Rome to Tradition. This refers to *apostolical Tradition*, by

120

which is meant the supposed sayings and doings of Christ and His apostles, not recorded in Scripture, but said to have been handed down orally from generation to another; and *ecclesiastical Tradition*, by which is meant all the various acts and decisions of the Roman Church. Pallavacini, a Roman Catholic writer, tells us that, in regard to this question, there were in the Council of Trent, in the sixteenth century, 'almost as many opinions in the Council as there were heads.' After much dissension, they decided that 'Tradition is to be received with equal piety with Scripture'. Cardinal Robert Bellarmine (1542-1621), a great Roman Catholic controversialist and theologian, went further and declared: 'We shall endeavour to demonstrate that the Scriptures without the Traditions are neither sufficient nor *simply necessary*.'

More than this, the Creed of Pope Pius IV (1564), an authoritative document of the Roman Church, forbids anyone to interpret Scripture 'otherwise than according to the unanimous consent of the Fathers'. This means that no interpretation can be placed on Scripture unless all the Fathers are agreed upon it. There is, however, no such thing as a 'unanimous consent of the Fathers', as even eminent Roman Catholic writers showed in the days before the Council of Trent. Even if there were unanimous agreement among the Fathers, no layman could possibly collect these voluminous opinions on any one point. Hence laymen are virtually prohibited from interpreting the Scriptures by this order of Pope Pius IV.

The medieval Church taught that it was essential to salvation that men attain an absolutely correct statement of what the Scriptures did reveal about God and man and the relationship between them. They held also that the faith that saves was not trust in a Person but assent to correct propositions about God, the universe and the soul of man. Thus, the saving character

121

of the assent depended on the correctness of the propositions assented to. Now it is part of the creed of the Roman Church that the Church alone, speaking through popes and Councils, can tell what is the truth about God and the soul. Hence, men are entirely at the mercy of popes and Councils, and dare not form their own judgement. Thus it was that when Luther began studying the Bible in the convent at Erfurt, his friend, John Nathin, said to him, 'Brother Martin, let the Bible alone; read the old teachers; reading the Bible simply breeds unrest'.

Notwithstanding all that Roman Catholic authorities have said, popes and Councils have undoubtedly erred frequently in their judgements, and erred grievously. Their decisions were, after all, but the work of fallible mortals and bear the impress of that fact. They made so many rules that men were lost in the ecclesiastical labyrinths and were separated from God. Moreover, people were taught that salvation through the grace of God rested upon the efficacy of seven sacraments which could be administered by the priest alone, so that the Church members were completely dependent upon him, irrespective of the quality of his own life.

The Reformers swept away all this. They put the Word of God freely into the hands of the people, and so brought them directly to God through the Christ who is revealed in its pages and who saves to the uttermost without the mediation of human priests. In acting thus the Reformers were following the example of the Master who so often declared 'It is written', and who asked His hearers to take that as conclusive. He said to the Sadducees 'Ye do err, not knowing the scriptures' (Matt. 22:29), implying that they were culpable in not knowing them. Our Lord emphatically told the Jews to 'Search the scriptures' (John 5:39). In these and many other cases, Christ referred to the teaching of the Bible as clear, authoritative and final. In the

122

same way, the apostles appealed constantly to the declarations of Scripture as conclusive. See for example, Acts 15:15-18 and 28:23. It is thus a grievous mistake to assert, as does the Vatican, that the Bible is too difficult to be understood by the common man and must be interpreted only by the decisions of popes and Councils. The Holy Scriptures have messages which are clear even to a child, as well as messages for the greatest saints and theologians.

2. The Reformers asserted the principle of the right of private judgement.

They denied the right of any man, or body of men, to set themselves up as final interpreters of the truth. In their opinion the claim of infallibility, whether made for popes or Councils, rests on no foundation whatever, and has to be completely rejected. St Paul insisted that Christians should 'prove all things' (1 Thess. 5:21). They had their own responsibility to examine the facts. The need for the Protestant doctrine of private judgement will be seen if we look again at Tradition as received in the Roman Church. The amount of matter which is included under the term Tradition is prodigious. It embraces thirty-five volumes of the Greek and Latin Fathers (whose 'unanimous consent' is supposed to be necessary to determine the meaning of any point in Scripture), numerous Papal Bulls, ten folio volumes of Decretals, thirty-one volumes of Acts of Councils, and fifty-one volumes of the sayings and doings of the saints. It would be the work of a lifetime for even a brilliant scholar to master all this, and yet the Council of Trent (1545-63) declared that 'Tradition is to be received with equal piety with Scripture.' The only sensible course is to exercise our own judgement, as the Reformers did, and reject this claim for Tradition. To exercise private judgement does not mean that we can believe what we like, no matter how irrational it may be. We must decide according to sound reason and logic, and common sense as well. It is also true that the more we have of the grace of God, the clearer our understanding of spiritual things will be.

3. The Scottish, like the Continental Reformers, emphasized strongly the priesthood of all believers.

Apart from the doctrine of the final authority of Scripture, this was the most basic principle of the Reformation. Luther had sought pardon for sin by following the path of extreme asceticism. He had been so punctilious in observing fasts and penances and scrupulously carrying out the whole routine of monastic observances, that he had become known for miles around as a most outstanding 'saint'. He knew, however, that he had not found what he sought, and there was no peace in his soul. In climbing Pilate's stairway in Rome on his hands and knees, he seemed to hear the words ringing in his ears 'The just shall live by his faith'. He then cast himself unreservedly on the mercy of God in Christ Jesus by the grace of the Most High. A new life came surging into his soul, completely changing him and giving him the certainty and peace which had hitherto eluded him. He was indeed renewed by the power of God and henceforth his watchword was 'justification by faith alone'.

Luther had been taught that he must come to the priest, confess all his sins, do penance according to the priest's instructions, impose sufferings on himself, sleep on stone floors, be whipped, give alms, repeat so many *Ave Marias*, and so on. When all this was done, he believed that the priests could absolve him. He had been told that inside the Roman Church alone was salvation, that only through its Sacraments could the grace of God come. Through the grace infused at

Baptism, original sin, and actual sins committed up till then, were washed away; and so with the other six Sacraments, each of them brought grace when ministered by the priest. Without him there was no chance of entering heaven, for he was the channel through which grace flowed. It is no wonder that the priestly caste had such a prominent place in the thoughts of the people.

Luther and the other Reformers came to realize that this was not the way of salvation pictured in the New Testament. They awakened to the fact that, as the 'veil of the temple was rent in twain from the top to the bottom' (Matt. 27:51) at the moment when Christ died on Calvary, and a way was thus opened into the most holy place which hitherto had been closed to all but the high priest, so, through the death of Christ, all believers can enter into the holiest of heaven above by the 'new and living way which He hath consecrated for us' (Heb. 10:19-20). Every believer had now come to enjoy the privileges of priesthood (Rev. 1: 6, 10) and could draw near to God 'in full assurance of faith' needing no other priest than Jesus, our great High Priest, who had offered Himself a sacrifice on the cross to take away our sins. No ecclesiastical ceremonies were required, nothing but the humble, believing acceptance by the truly penitent of the salvation wrought out by Christ (see Heb. 10:21-22). Through the acceptance of this truth by the Reformers, the special power of the ordained priest was broken, for all true believers were now made priests themselves. What Harnack wrote concerning Luther may be said of all who are justified by faith alone: 'Rising above all anxieties and terrors, above all ascetic devices, above all directions of theology, above all interventions of hierarchy and Sacraments, Luther ventures to lay hold of God Himself in Christ, and in this act of faith, which he recognized as God's work, his whole being obtained stability and firmness, nay, even a personal joy and certainty, which no medieval Christian had ever possessed.[1]

Through the Reformers, men came to know once again what every Christian knew in the early ages of the Church, that it was not through an earthly priest that regeneration came, that the priest's ministration of baptism did not of itself wash away sin, and that it was God alone who could give absolution from our guilt. All such provision for the needs of mankind came from the Eternal Father, through the merits of the Redeemer, and not from the words and actions of any fallible, mortal man.

In no place was the doctrine of the priesthood of all believers more whole-heartedly accepted than in the Reformed Church of Scotland. Not only did this free the land from priestcraft with its attendant evils, but it produced the Presbyterian conception that the government of the Church is equally in the hands of ministers and elders. It freed the land for a time from the curse of clericalism and greatly strengthened the belief that before God there are no distinctions of caste or class.

4. Like their Reformed brethren on the continent, the Scottish divines maintained strongly that nothing should be introduced into the worship or doctrine of the Church but what is expressly authorized in the Holy Scriptures.

In this respect the Scottish church differed from the Lutheran and the Anglican. The leaders of those churches acted upon the principle that anything not actually forbidden in the Bible could be introduced into the Church, if such a course should appear desirable. At first sight there appears to be little

---

1.   A. Harnack, *History of Dogma*, VII, p. 183.

difference between the two views, but in reality the difference is great. Had the principle adopted by the Scottish Reformers been acted upon in the early centuries, the Church would never have fallen into the grave errors and corruption of pre-Reformation days.

In laying down their principle, the authors of *The First Book of Discipline*[2] began by declaring that in the Books of the Old and New Testaments 'are all thing necessary for the instruction of the Church, and to make the man of God perfect,' and these things 'are sufficiently expressed'. Here is a clear declaration that in the Church the Word of God should prevail, not Tradition or anything else which the wit of man can conceive. They proceed to give examples of the kind of thing which can be introduced when the opposite principle is followed and men are at liberty to introduce what is not actually *forbidden*.

> By the contrary doctrine, we understand whatsoever men, by Laws, Councils, or Constitutions have imposed upon the consciences of men, without the expressed commandment of God's Word: such as be vows of chastity, foreswearing of marriage, binding of men and women to several and disguised apparels, to the superstitious observance of fasting days, difference of meat for conscience sake, prayer for the dead; and keeping of holy days of certain Saints commanded by man, such as be all those that the Papists have invented, as the Feasts (as they term them) of Apostles, Martyrs, Virgins, of Christmas, Circumcision, Epiphany, Purification, and other fond feasts of our Lady. Which things, because in God's Scriptures they neither have commandment nor assurance, we judge them utterly to be abolished from this Realm ... [3]

---

2.   See pp. 135-48 for an account of this work.

3.   *The First Book of Discipline* (in Dunlop's *Confessions*, p. 519).

Had this rule been acted upon faithfully it would have saved the Church from the serious consequences of many human vagaries and from the manifestations of the pride and pomp which have so often weakened the good cause. The modern Churchman, who is not very sure where he is going, might do worse than ponder the significance of this old principle which at one time was so greatly honoured in the Reformed Churches.

5. *The Scottish Reformers returned to the apostolicity of the early Church.*

The claim of the Church of Rome is that it is not only Catholic but apostolic. The contention of the Reformers was that the Roman Church had departed so far from the teachings and practice of the early centuries that it had become pathetically different from the apostles' Church. In the primitive Church the leaders were plain men who had no pretensions to worldly glory and power. A complete change came over the Church in the course of the Middle Ages and there was scarcely any limit to the pride and pomp of its representatives. Pope Gregory VII (Hildebrand) (1073-1085) declared that, as vicar of Christ and representative of Peter, he could give or take away 'empires, kingdoms, duchies, marquisates, and the possessions of all men.' Everyone on earth must acknowledge him. At a later period, Pope Boniface VIII (1294-1303) insisted most strongly that all temporal rulers were subject to him, and wrote in his bull *'Unam Sanctam'*, 'We declare, state, define and pronounce that for every human creature to be subject to the Roman pope is altogether necessary to salvation.' Further than this the claims of arrogance could not go. At the Reformation all such claims were rejected. The pope was declared to have no more authority than any other bishop, and in the Reformed Churches, of which the Scottish branch was probably the most thoroughgoing, the parity of all ministers was once again proclaimed, and elders were given equal power in the courts of the Church.

It is worthwhile recalling some of the ways in which the Church had departed from apostolic practice. Shortly before the middle of the third century Cyprian of Carthage brought into the Church the non-Christian conception of the minister as a *sacrificing priest*. The idea gained ground gradually but surely, and at last, in 1215 the doctrine of Transubstantiation was officially proclaimed in the Roman Church. There is no suggestion of such a doctrine in the New Testament. The very idea that a priest can change the bread and wine in the communion into the very body and blood, soul and divinity of the Lord Jesus, and offer Him again on the altar as 'a propitiatory sacrifice for the living and the dead' is absolutely foreign to apostolic teaching.

Then again, there were no images and no pictures of Christ or the angels in churches during the first three centuries. When they were first introduced, the Council of Elvira in Spain protested in 306. A Council at Constantinople in 730 expressly forbade them, and so did the Council of Frankfurt in 794 with the help of Charlemagne, although the pope strongly favoured their use. The custom, however, became universal and throughout the Church images were worshipped. Nothing could be less apostolic.

We see the same lamentable departure from apostolic practice in regard to purgatory, the adoration of the Host, the adoration of the Virgin Mary, the worship of saints and angels, to cite only a few examples. Because of such things the claim of the Church of Rome to be apostolic became a misuse of words. At the Reformation, with the return to New Testament teaching and practice, the Church became once more *apostolic* in its attitude and such rites and observances as were foreign to the spirit of the gospel were swept away.

11

THE SCOTS CONFESSION AND THE
FIRST BOOK OF DISCIPLINE

The Scots Confession

The Scots Confession deals with the same kind of questions as the other Creeds or Symbols of the various Protestant Churches. It contains twenty-five Articles in all and sets forth the doctrinal position of the Church on such themes as God, Creation, Original Sin, the Incarnation, Election, Christ's Death, the Resurrection, the Church, Good Works, the Sacraments, the Authority of the Scriptures and so on. Although much shorter, it is in spirit and content much the same as *The Westminster Confession of Faith* which was officially adopted in its place by the Church of Scotland in 1647. The declaration was then made by the Assembly that *The Westminster Confession* was received as 'in nothing contrary' to the former. *The Scots Confession* was prepared, as we have seen, in a remarkably short space of time, while the Westminster document was drawn up by a large number of very learned divines over a period of about three and a half years. It is not surprising, then, to find out that the latter is more mature, more terse, and more calm and judicial. Nevertheless the old Confession had decided merits of its own. It is homely in style, free from metaphysical distinctions, and concentrates on the really important points, which it brings home to the reader with clearness and remarkable success. It is an excellent summary of Reformed doctrine, and Professor A.F. Mitchell of St Andrews has made out a strong case for the thesis that, although not so full, it is yet, basically, as Reformed as the Confession which replaced it.[1]

As shown in the previous chapter, the teachings of *The Scots Confession* and other authoritative doctrinal works of the Reformers were based four-square on the Bible. Thus chapter XVIII declares 'for the doctrine taught in our kirks is contained in the written word of God, to wit, in the Books of the Old and New Testaments.' In the preface there is a humble acknowledgement of human frailty, and the authors solemnly intimate 'that if any man will not in this our confession any article or sentence repugnant to God's holy word, that it would please him of his gentleness, and for Christian charities' sake, to admonish us of the same in writing; and we upon our honour and fidelity, by God's grace, do promise unto him satisfaction from the mouth of God, that is from His Holy Scriptures, or else reformation of them which he shall prove to be amiss.'[2] Clearly, for them the Bible was the final authority.

It is worth noting how careful all the branches of the Protestant Church were in framing their Confessions in the sixteenth century. They were anxious to be clear in their own minds as to what they believed, and anxious also to be plainly understood in the message they proclaimed to the world. They were men of deep convictions and spoke with unwavering confidence. Like Paul, they believed that 'if the trumpet give an uncertain sound' nothing but confusion can take place in the battle (1 Cor. 14:8). Hence the clarity, force and persuasiveness of their utterances.

We can give only a few examples of the style and teaching of the Confession. Chapter III, 'On Original Sin', is a good

---

1.   A.F. Mitchell, *The Scottish Reformation*, pp. 116-20 (Baird Lecture, 1899).

2.   Dunlop's *Confessions*, II, pp. 17, 18.

specimen. It shows how through transgression 'the image of God was utterly defaced in man'. Adam's descendants became 'enemies to God, slaves to satan, and servants to sin'. Only regeneration, wrought from on high, by the Holy Ghost, can save men from the everlasting death which has laid hold of all. The Holy Ghost works 'in the hearts of the elect of God an assured faith in the promise of God'. Thus, we apprehend Christ 'with the graces and benefits promised in Him'. This is sound Reformed teaching. It is far more. It is entirely in line with the doctrine of St Augustine early in the fifth century, and this in turn was based upon the Epistles of St Paul.

Chapter XII presents us with the remedy for the sad spiritual corruption just described. As God 'created us, when we were not', so the Holy Ghost sanctifies and regenerates us without any respect for any merit in us. As we cannot claim any glory for ourselves in our creation, so in regard to regeneration and sanctification, it is only God, who began the good work in us, who can carry it on. It is to the praise of 'His undeserved grace'. We are dead in trespasses and sins and can be made alive spiritually only by the power of the Holy Spirit. Many passages from the Bible are quoted to support these statements.

Chapter VII states that, since the Spirit alone can quicken those dead in sin, God must elect those to be regenerated. The following chapter tells how 'the eternal God and Father' of His grace alone, 'elected us in Christ Jesus His Son, before the foundation of the world'. Again, the doctrine is supported by many Scripture quotations.[3] Here we have a profound mystery which ought to be treated with great reverence and caution. It is easy to cavil at this solemn doctrine; it is not so easy to unravel the profound mysteries involved. God alone can do so.

3.   See Dunlop's *Confessions*, II, p. 32; II, pp. 60, 61.

Chapter XV contains a really admirable exposition of 'Justification by faith alone', sometimes described as 'the article of a standing or a falling Church'. It was basic in the teachings of the Reformers. Chapters XVI and XVIII deal with the doctrine of the Church. As in other Reformed Church Creeds, it is the Invisible Church which is stressed. It is 'a company and multitude of men chosen of God, who rightly worship and embrace Him, by true faith in Christ Jesus, who is the only Head of the same Kirk ... which Kirk is Catholic, that is universal, because it contains the Elect of all ages and tongues ... who have communion and society with God the Father, and with His Son Christ Jesus, through the sanctification of His Holy Spirit.'[4] This is a broad, tolerant view of the Church Universal embracing every section. At the Reformation and long afterwards the Reformed Churches practiced intercommunion. The Anglican Church did the same, and it was only in the time of Archbishop Laud that exclusiveness entered which, at times, has made it difficult to allow men from other denominations to take communion. Open communion is still the practice in nearly all Presbyterian Churches. The Invisible Church becomes visible in those who profess faith in Christ and follow Him, but God alone can know for certain how many members of the Visible Church are also members of the Invisible which is the true Church of God.[5]

There are, however, certain evidences as to who are genuine believers and who are not. There are also 'notes' which show whether any branch of the professing Church is really part of the true Church of Christ. *The Scots Confession* declares it is not 'antiquity, usurped title, lineal descent, place appointed, nor

---

4.   See Dunlop's *Confessions*, II, p. 60.

5.   Dunlop, *op. cit.*, p. 8.

multitude of men approving' which made a true Church. The positive 'notes' are: (1) 'The true preaching of the Word of God'. It is not any kind of preaching. It must be in accordance with the Word, not the preaching of human vagaries and fancies. (2) 'The right administration of the Sacraments' to seal the truth on the hearts and lives of men. The only Sacraments are Baptism and the Lord's Supper. (3) 'Ecclesiastical discipline uprightly ministered as God's Word prescribes'.[6] The aim of the discipline was to repress vice and nourish virtue. The moral principles of the gospel had to be maintained and propagated. Those living scandalous lives must be lovingly admonished but as a last resort they must be removed from the membership to preserve the purity of the Church. The discipline was rigid, for it was necessary to purge the Church from long-standing iniquities.

Chapter XXIV deals with relations of Church and State. 'Powers and authorities', it says, 'are ordained for the manifestation of God's glory, and for the singular profit of humanity'. Those in authority should, therefore, be 'loved, honoured, and feared'. Both the Church and State are ordained of God, the one for the spiritual sphere, the other for the secular. They should co-operate mutually for the welfare of the people, but the one must not invade the sphere of the other. It was Knox who originated this conception of the co-ordinate authority of Church and State, so well known in Scotland now.[7]

The First Book of Discipline

The same six ministers who were asked by Parliament to draw up the Confession were also requested to draw up a statement showing how the Church should be governed and how discipline should be exercised. Their work is known as *The First Book of*

---

6.   Dunlop, *op. cit.*, II, pp. 66-8.

7.   'The Civil Magistrate', in Dunlop's *Confessions*, II pp. 90-3.

Discipline or *The Policie and Discipline of the Church*, which is set forth in sixteen chapters. It is a remarkable document revealing better than anything else the statesmanlike qualities of the leading ministers, and their amazing far-sightedness. Because of the recommendations made regarding the patrimony of the Church, *The First Book of Discipline* was never approved by Parliament, for many of the barons had taken possession of vast territories belonging to the Church. A good number of the nobles and burgesses, however, signed the documents privately and promised to forward its aims by every means in their power. It is pleasing to notice among the signatories men like Lord James Stewart (Earl of Moray), Archibald, fifth Earl of Argyll, The Earl of Glencairn and Lord Ochiltree. It was men of this type who really counted in the great Reformation movement, not the self-seekers who supported a cause only when they were assured of it success.

The chief headings in the *Book of Discipline* and the *Book of Common Order* are as follows:

a. *The Office-Bearers of the Church*
In *The Book of Common Order* drawn up by Knox in 1556 for use in his congregation at Geneva, the permanent office-bearers of the Christian Church are described as ministers, elders, deacons and doctors. The last-named would correspond, more or less, to professors or lecturers in our modern theological colleges. The apostles held a very special office and had no successors. *The Book of Discipline* recognized the offices of minister, elder, and deacon as permanent in the Church, but added two *temporary* offices to meet the abnormal situation existing immediately after the Reformation. These were the offices of 'superintendent' and 'reader'.

1.   Ministers. The position and functions of Presbyterian ministers were very much as at present. Each congregation had the right to elect its own minister, but ministers had to be examined by the Church as to their fitness for the office. They were expected not to 'live riotously, nor yet avariciously'. It was regarded as intolerable 'that ministers should be boarded in common ale-houses or taverns'. It is obvious that the Reformed Church wished to save its ministers from temptations which proved too much for some clergy of the old Church.[8] In view of more recent practice, it is interesting to note that *The First Book of Discipline* disapproves of the laying on of hands at ordinations and inductions of ministers. 'Albeit the apostles used the imposition of hands, yet seeing the miracle is ceased, the using of the ceremony we judge is not necessary.'[9]

There are certain pointed references to the duties of ministers. The gospel must be 'truly and openly preached in every church and assembly of this realm', and in this case they meant by 'gospel' the whole range of divine truth.[10] No man who is 'unable to edify the Church by wholesome Doctrine' is to be admitted to the ministry, or 'retained in ecclesiastical administration.'[11] It is clear that ministers who could not preach were not wanted. Thus, the Sacraments could not be 'rightly administered by him in whose mouth God hath put no sermon of exhortation'. Again, we are told that to have a minister who cannot preach and can only read homilies prepared by others (as was actually done in some countries) was 'alike to have no minister at all, and to have an idol in the place of a true minister, yea, and in some cases it is worse', for many content themselves with having this vain shadow and do not

---

8. *The Book of Discipline*, chapter 7.

9. *Op. cit.*, chapter 4.

10. Dunlop's *Confessions*, II, p. 518.

11. Dunlop, *op. cit.*, II, p. 526.

seek for a real minister.[12] This insistence on a high standard of preaching is remarkable in view of the very great dearth of ministers at the time.

2. *Superintendents*. The fewness of ministers is shown by the fact that at the first General Assembly held on 20 December 1560 there were present only six ministers and thirty-six elders. It is true that a few more were in the country but the total was lamentably small for supplying religious ordinances to all Scotland. To supply the deficiency, 'readers' were appointed to read the Scriptures and the common prayers in church on the Lord's Day. They were not allowed to preach until they proved their ability, and they could not administer the Sacraments. To supervise the work of these readers ten or twelve 'godly and learned men' were chosen as 'superintendents'. One was appointed to each of the provinces, corresponding more or less to the old dioceses. They had to visit the congregations of their area regularly, preach at least thrice every week, administer the Sacraments where there was no ordained minister, see that discipline was maintained and promote sound Christian living among the people. High Churchmen have argued that the Scottish superintendent was simply 'the bishop done into Latin'. We may grant that there were certain resemblances between the functions of the superintendent and the diocesan bishop; but there were, at the same time, enormous differences. As, somewhat incongruously, strenuous efforts have been made by Episcopalians to prove that John Knox and his contemporaries in the ministry were quite prepared to accept Church government by some kind of hierarchy which would include bishops, the question is worth

12.   Dunlop, *op.cit.*, II, p. 530.

examining. Professor A. F. Mitchell has shown conclusively that the differences between the position of superintendents and that of bishops were basic.[13]

(i)   A bishop had to be consecrated by three, or at least two, bishops in lineal succession, as was supposed from the apostles. The superintendent could be set apart by a simple presbyter.

(ii) The duties of the bishop could be devolved only on one of his own order. The duties of the superintendent were often devolved on an ordinary minister when appointed by the General Assembly.

(iii) Preaching was not a main duty of bishops but it was of the superintendents.

(iv) A bishop could negative a decision of his clergy in Synod and could not be put under discipline by them. The superintendent was simply permanent moderator of the Synod and was bound to give effect to its decisions like any other minister. He could be charged and punished for neglect of duty by the Synod.

(v)   The superintendent was subject to the General Assembly composed of ministers and elders. He sat in that court with no more power there than one of its humblest members. Moreover, the office of superintendent was only temporary, for the duration of that time of difficulty.

It has also to be borne in mind that Knox belonged to the school of Calvin who, as early as 1541, laid down in his *Ordinances* the Presbyterian form of Church government. Further, although the

13.   See A. F. Mitchell, *The Scottish Reformation*, pp. 155-8.

Scottish Reformer gladly co-operated with evangelical bishops in England, he never accepted their polity, and on this ground refused the bishopric of Rochester and strongly denounced attempts to bring the Scottish Church under the government of bishops. His party in Frankfurt refused to have a bishop.

3. *Elders*. They have an important place in *The First Book of Discipline*. They were to assist the minister in all public affairs of the Church: to help in judging and deciding causes, in giving admonition to the licentious and in helping to improve the manners and conversation of all men in their charge. They were the members of the Kirk Session who, under the presidency of the minister, guided the spiritual affairs of the local congregation. They, like the deacons, were elected for one year only, by free vote of the congregation, but could be re-elected. They had to be men of the best knowledge of God's Word, of cleanest life and the most honest conversation which could be found.

To us, a surprising feature of *The First Book of Discipline* is that it laid upon elders the duty of taking heed to 'the life, manners, diligence, and study of the minister'. They were to admonish and correct him where desirable, and if worthy of deposition to proceed against him in the Church courts.[14] This clearly shows the parity of ministers and elders in accordance with New Testament teaching. The minister is simply an elder set apart for special work.

4. *Deacons*. Their function was to look after the financial interests of the Church, receive rents and gather alms, and distribute the same as might be appointed by the Church.

5. *Readers*. As we have seen, readers were an important element in the Church when, following the Reformation, there

14. *The First Book of Discipline*. See Dunlop's *Confessions*, II, p. 578.

was so great a dearth of ministers. We have already noted their functions.[15] If they showed themselves capable they could be raised to be grade of 'exhorter' and be allowed not only to read the Scriptures but to expound them. Many readers, on securing a better education, were appointed schoolmasters, and not a few applied themselves so diligently to study that they qualified for entry into the ordained ministry. It says much for the vitality of the new Church that, starting out with about twelve ministers in 1560, the cause grew so rapidly that in 1567 there were 1048 churches, 257 ordained ministers, 455 readers and 151 exhorters. It is significant that by this date the number of superintendents was reduced to five. The same rate of progress continued, and soon there was no need for either superintendents or readers because of the remarkable increase in ordained ministers.

b. Church Government

The First Book of Discipline does not lay down specifically that the Church must be governed by kirk sessions, presbyteries, synods and General Assemblies, but it is easily seen that these are assumed in a rudimentary form. Professor John Cunningham points out that (1) the minister is required to meet at stated times with his elders and deacons. This was the origin of the *kirk session*. (2) The ministers within six miles of the larger towns had to meet weekly at what were called 'prophesyings' or 'exercises'. They joined with other believers in the study and interpretation of the Scriptures. Each was allowed to express freely his views for the edification of the brethren, but sermonizing was forbidden. It was a time for considering doubts and for fraternal admonition. Through

---

15.   See under *Superintendents*, p. 138.

these 'exercises' the gifts of the brethren were discovered, and made available to the Church. In these meetings is found the origin of the *presbytery*. Queen Elizabeth was quick to perceive this tendency in England and forbade the 'prophesyings', in spite of the expostulations of her godly Archbishop, Grindal. (3) The superintendent had to meet with the ministers of his province, and so we have an embryo *synod*. (4) For the beginning, the Scottish Church had the *General Assembly*. It was representative of the various parts of the country and the ministers and elders each had their place. It would be difficult to exaggerate the importance of this noble institution in the history of the Scottish people. To this day it continues to express the religious and moral ideals of the nation, and it is safe to say that in no other country in the world does an ecclesiastical court attract so much attention and interest as does the General Assembly in Scotland.

At first, the Kirk Session, as on the continent, exercised authority over several congregations. For example, in Edinburgh, Glasgow, Dundee and Perth, one Kirk Session ruled all the believers. It was often called the 'lesser presbytery' or 'eldership'. Afterwards it became known as the 'greater eldership' or 'classical presbytery' as we know it, and it absorbed the 'exercises' or prophesyings. The kirk session was then left to rule the local congregation, as it does now.

c. *Worship and Discipline*
The order of service on the Lord's Day was very much as at present. In accordance with the custom of the Reformed Churches on the continent at that time (as distinct from the Lutherans), only the metrical psalms were used in public praise and there was no organ accompaniment. This continued to be the general practice in Presbyterian Churches until 1861

when the Church of Scotland sanctioned the use of hymns. From then onwards the use of both hymns and instrumental music gradually came to be approved in the Presbyterian Churches throughout the world, except in some of the smaller bodies where the practice of the Scottish Reformers in this connection is still clung to tenaciously.

The Reformers recommended that in large towns there should be sermon, or common prayers, with reading of the Scriptures every day, and that in small towns this be done on at least one day beside Sunday. 'The Sunday must be straitly kept, both before and after noon, in all towns.' Before noon the Word was preached and the Sacraments administered. In the afternoon the children were examined publicly in their Catechism before the people, and the minister was enjoined to 'take great diligence' to see that the people understood the doctrines involved.

All holy days, except the Lord's Day, were abolished as having no biblical warrant. Only those who have lived in a Roman Catholic country realize what a burden saints' days can be and what a hindrance to normal activities. All vows of celibacy and the assumption of special religious apparel were declared to be sinful.

In baptism, water only was to be used as symbolizing the truth that sinners are cleansed through the purifying effect of Christ's sacrifice applied by the Holy Spirit. The use of oil, salt, wax, spittle, conjuration, crossing, as practised in the Roman Church, was forbidden, because these were inventions of men and suggested that the New Testament ordinance was imperfect.

The Lord's Supper was administered very much as it is done at present in Presbyterian Churches, except that there were no individual communion cups. Candidates for communion were required to repeat the Lord's Prayer, the Ten Commandments, and the Creed before being received into Church membership.

Both the bread and wine had to be given to the communicants, unlike the Roman Church where the cup is denied to the laity. *The Book of Discipline* laid down that 'The Table of the Lord is most rightly ministered when it approacheth most nigh to Christ's own action,' at the last Supper.[16] Transubstantiation was, of course, strongly condemned.

Before the Reformation, at least some Protestants in Scotland used the Second Prayer Book of Edward VI, but considerable latitude was then allowed in its use. It is certain that John Knox, when in England, did not use this Prayer Book in its full extent if, indeed, he used it at all. After the Reformation, *The Book of Common Order*, often called erroneously *Knox's Liturgy*, came to be used instead of the English book for it was approved by *The First Book of Discipline* in 1560 and by the General Assembly in 1564. It was intended as a guide and aid to ministers in conducting services, but not intended to be slavishly followed. It was certainly not observed as a rigid liturgy, every word of which must be repeated. Several times the injunction is given that the minister shall use a certain prayer, or one *like in effect*, or *such like*.[17] It is insisted that the Holy Spirit must be sought in prayer, and in one place the minister is instructed to pray as the Spirit *shall move his heart*.[18] Calderwood, Row and others, who greatly valued the *Book of Common Order*, have made it clear that the book was intended to be a directory, and that free and extemporary prayer was encouraged. In view of the attempts frequently made to present John Knox as virtually a ritualist, it is worthwhile keeping this in view.

---

16. 'The First Book of Discipline' in Dunlop's *Confessions*, II, pp. 520-2.

17. 'The Book of Common Order' in Dunlop's *Confessions*, II, pp. 417, 421.

18. Dunlop, *op. cit.*, II, p. 426.

d. The Patrimony of the Kirk

It is well known that the Roman Church before the Reformation owned about half the wealth of Scotland. A great part of this wealth consisted of extensive territories belonging to the monasteries. When it became apparent that the Reformation was going to succeed, many of these lands were passed over by the ecclesiastical occupiers to secular owners. Other lands were taken possession of illegally by ruthless and selfish barons.

As the Roman Church in Scotland had virtually ceased to exist in 1560, the question arose: What was to be done with the vast revenues of the Church? The framers of *The Book of Discipline*, under the leadership of John Knox, proposed that the income of the Church be divided into three parts: one for the maintenance of a gospel ministry, another for the promotion of education throughout the land, and a third for the support of the poor, as the Church of Christ had always regarded the care of the poor as a sacred trust. This was very much in line with the purposes for which these funds had been given to the Church originally. The whole scheme reflects great credit on John Knox. Even his severest critics must admit that the plan now presented to Parliament showed him to be possessed of great gifts of head and heart. No grander scheme has ever been proposed for the welfare of Scotland. It revealed outstanding statesmanship as well as a determination to promote religion and virtue.

1. The Ministry. The proposals detailed for the maintenance of the ministry were far from extravagant and certainly not on a higher scale than the Scottish people have ever thought reasonable. Some provision was also suggested for the education of their families.

2.   *Education.* After a preamble in which the great value of a virtuous education and godly upbringing is stressed, the scheme is presented in detail. In towns, the Church must appoint a schoolmaster, 'such an one as could, at least, teach Grammar and the Latin tongue'. In country parishes, the minister or reader must taken charge of a school 'to instruct the children in the first rudiments'. 'In every notable town' there must be erected a College or High School 'in which the Arts, at least Logic and Rhetoric, together with the Tongues, be read by sufficient Masters for whom honest stipends must be appointed'. Provision must be made for the children of the poor who are not able of themselves to pay for the education of their families. Finally, the universities must 'be replenished with those that be apt to learning'. People of every class, of whatever estate, must be compelled to bring up their children in learning and virtue. The rich must be compelled to educate their children at their own expense, but the children of the poor must be assisted in the pursuit of learning whenever they have aptitudes 'so that the Commonwealth' may benefit by them. Remarkably full and wise regulations are laid down for the guidance of the schools and universities, the nature of the curriculum, the salaries and so on.

The gibe has often been hurled at Churchmen that they are inept in matters of business. Anyone who reads The First Book of Discipline, especially on the subject of education and the care of the poor, can see the work of six ministers who were clear-headed, far-sighted, and possessed of admirable business qualities. It is astonishing to see these men in 1560 laying down principles which only in the twentieth century have come to be universally accepted in our land. Far ahead of their age they advocated compulsory education, and a scheme whereby the lad of ability, though poor, would be helped on from the humble parish school to the university. The shocking greed of the nobles gravely hindered but did not destroy the scheme. The Church did what it could, and never lost sight of Knox's ideal of 'a kirk and a school in every parish'. It was not fully realized in regard to schools until the last quarter of the eighteenth century. The record of the Church in Scotland in promoting education is without equal, and caused the Scottish peasantry to be the best educated in the world. As an example of what the Reformed Church ideal of popular education did for Scotland, we may recall that in the year 1800 there were 1,000 students in Oxford and Cambridge combined, the only universities in England. Scotland had four universities and in Edinburgh alone there were 993 students. In 1830 the English universities had less than 3,000 students, while the Scottish universities had 4,400 in spite of the fact that the population of England was eight times that of Scotland. What would the position of Scotland have been if the misguided nobles had not grabbed the revenues which John Knox had designated for education?

3. *The Poor*. The Book of Discipline pleaded nobly also for the peasantry who had formerly been oppressed by the ruthless exactions of the clergy but were now as cruelly treated by the lords and lairds who claimed the teinds formerly exacted by the Roman Church. With great courage it was urged that the earls and barons should 'live upon their just rents' so that the poor should receive some 'comfort and relaxation'. The demand was made that the teinds be completely demolished and also such miserable charges as those for death dues and Easter offerings which were a burden to the poor. Professor Mitchell writes: 'The history of the world, the history of the Christian Church, has few passages more noble than this, where these poor ministers, not yet assured of decent provision

for their own maintenance, boldly undertake the patronage of the peasantry, and say they would rather suffer themselves than ask that teinds should be exacted from those who had been so long ground down.'[19]

Parliament, as we have already seen, refused to approve *The Book of Discipline*.[20] Some, like William Maitland of Lethington, openly sneered at its provisions. To others it was odious because it rebuked their licentiousness. The failure to approve the financial schemes for the maintenance of the ministry, the promotion of education, and the help of the poor, was a deplorable mistake on the part of Parliament. The Church in its poverty struggled manfully on, making what provision it could for these worthy objects.

---

19. A.F. Mitchell, *The Scottish Reformation*, p. 180.

20. See p. 135.

1 2

THE QUEEN RETURNS

On 5 December 1560, when Mary Queen of Scots was only eighteen years of age, Francis II of France, her delicate young husband, died. This event produced mighty changes for both France and Scotland. The queen's uncles, the Duke of Guise and the Cardinal of Lorraine, had led poor Francis into a bloody persecution of the Huguenots. The situation had become very serious, if not indeed dangerous, throughout the country. With the death of the king, the Guise family lost their evil power for the time being, and influence passed into the hands of the Queen Mother, Catherine de Medici. In Scotland there was a distinct sense of relief. There had been a growing fear that, with Mary married to the king of France, the land would be again completely dominated by that country in both civil and ecclesiastical matters.

Almost immediately, in spite of her grief, rumours began to circulate freely about plans to marry Mary to one of the many aspirants for her hand. Among those most persistently mentioned were Don Carlos, the heir of Philip II of Spain, the most powerful monarch in the world at that time; the Earl of Arran, a fervent Protestant, very close in the line of succession to the Scottish throne; the kings of Denmark and Sweden, and others. The question of the queen's second marriage was a very serious one for Scotland. Mary herself seems to have indicated from the beginning that she would marry the man who 'could best uphold her greatness'.

The Scots were anxious for the return of their queen to her own country. In April 1561 two outstanding personalities sped off to France to negotiate with her. One was John Lesley, afterwards Bishop of Ross, who represented the interests of the Roman Church. The other was Lord James Stewart, the queen's half-brother, who represented the Protestant party which was then dominant in Scotland. Lesley got there first and saw her at Vitry on her way to Nancy in Lorraine. He warned her in the strongest terms against Lord James who was, he said, seeking the utter destruction of the Catholic religion. He urged her to land in Aberdeen where Catholic nobles would meet her with 20,000 men and lead her to Edinburgh. Next day, Lord James overtook her at St Dizier and was kindly received. His evident frankness and sincerity made an impression and she decided to recognize the Protestant party in Scotland, at least for a time. She and the Cardinal of Lorraine did their utmost to win over Lord James to the Roman Church, holding out to him the most tempting inducements; but he was unflinchingly loyal both to the Protestant cause and to the alliance with England.

Throckmorton, the English ambassador in Paris, had heard that the King of Spain had advised Queen Mary to temporize in matters of religion at first; later, she could take drastic measures against pertinacious heretics, when he would be in a position to help her. According to Sir James Melville, various Frenchmen including d'Oysel who knew Scotland intimately, advised her to hope for the English succession, to bide her time and accommodate herself discreetly and gently to her Scottish subjects, and to be most familiar with Lord James, Argyll, Lethington and Grange of the Protestant party. This was unquestionably her policy for some time after she returned to Scotland. Her plan was to win the confidence of the Scots, gradually to undermine the Protestant position, and, at an opportune time, to re-establish the old religion.[1] Lord James, satisfied with his interview with his half-sister, hurried home to make arrangements for her reception when she should arrive.

We shall never understand the tragic story of Mary of Scotland if we do not remember the following facts.

1. She had the misfortune to lose her father, James V, when only one week old; and when still under six she was separated from her mother to be sent to a convent in France. There she was reared under the influence of what has often been described as 'the most licentious court in Europe'.

2. Under the direction of the bigoted House of Guise she was taught from childhood to distrust, if not to hate, all Protestants and even in her teens she had seen some of them cruelly done to death at the instigation of her uncles.

3. It was the period of the Council of Trent which, under the direction of the Jesuits, had set in motion the Counter Reformation. The Roman Church was determined, by hook or by crook, to win back what had been lost. It was a time of endless intrigue and constant plotting, when emissaries from the Vatican went secretly hither and thither to organize opposition to the hated Protestant movement. Some of these emissaries were received in Holyrood Palace and privately lodged by Queen Mary.

4. She was trained from childhood in the belief that royalty had a divine prerogative to be absolutist and dictatorial;

---

1.   D. Hay Fleming, *Mary Queen of Scots*, p. 234, note 29.

and that, particularly in the matter of religion, subjects were bound to follow the sovereign. This idea was dominant at that time in the leading courts of Europe, but it was bound to bring Mary into violent collision with the Scottish Reformers with their more democratic ideals.

5.   The nobles of Scotland had never been very subservient to the monarch and were apt to be rebellious. In the period of Queen Mary they were particularly difficult and unrestrained. Dastardly plots, kidnappings and assassinations were common. It was truly a hard situation for a young queen to face.

When we consider all these facts, we can scarcely wonder that her life was one of sadness and tragedy. Over and above all this there was the fact that she was a beautiful and fascinating woman. Even today there are hundreds of thousands who feel that fascination. When she was alive there were very few men, apart from John Knox, who could withstand the spell of her feminine wiles. This was really her undoing for, conscious of her power, she followed courses which led to her ruin.

―――

The prospect of the queen's arrival caused much perturbation in Knox's mind, for he saw in the event great danger to the Protestant cause and the possible defeat of the plans for which he had laboured so intensely. No other man in Britain knew so well the realities of the European situation, and the attitude of France and Spain towards all who supported the Reformation. He was keenly alive to the plans of the French court for the destruction of his religion and was aware of the aims of the young queen and of her relatives on the continent. She, for her part, regarded the Reformer as the most dangerous man in her kingdom and vowed before she arrived that she would either banish him or refuse to dwell there herself, and she did her best to prejudice Queen Elizabeth against him. She might have saved herself the trouble, for the queen of England was already quite sufficiently prejudiced. Knox, for his part, was convinced that Mary ought not to be received as queen unless she agreed to conform to the laws of the land which Parliament had passed the previous year in regard to religion. This was not unreasonable. It has been customary in Great Britain, since the union of the Parliaments, to exact an oath from every new sovereign to maintain the Protestant faith. Many of the godly shared Knox's misgivings, but the politicians among the Protestants were prepared to compromise, and Lord James, while utterly opposed to her celebrating Mass publicly, maintained there could be no objection to her having it celebrated privately. John Knox, knowing well the nature of Mary's upbringing in the House of Guise, foresaw that she would not remain satisfied with this concession to practise her own religion in the Palace, but would use it to strengthen further the power of the Roman Church and bring her subjects again under its sway.

On 19 August 1561, the queen arrived at Leith and was joyously received by most of her subjects. She had been refused a safe passport by Queen Elizabeth because she had evaded signing the Treaty of Edinburgh in which Elizabeth was recognized as Queen of England. Mary claimed that she herself was Queen of England and had quartered the English armorial bearings upon her coat of arms. Elizabeth was furious, and English cruisers were in the Channel trying to intercept her but failed because of fog.

The Queen of Scotland reached her own land accompanied by no less than three of her Guise uncles, the Duke d'Aumale, the Duke de Guise and the Marquis d'Elboeuf, as well as other French gentlemen. In the evening she was led to Holyrood Palace. Bonfires blazed on the hills, and Knox tells us that 'a company of most honest men, with instruments of music, gave their salutations at her chamber window'. The queen was courteous enough to express keen appreciation of their performance and asked them to return again, but Bantome, the chronicler, declared the music was atrocious and that it was performed on wretched fiddles and rebecs. With great diligence the lords repaired to her from all quarters to express their loyalty, and, according to Knox's narrative, all was mirth and quietness until the next Sunday. On that day, however, the storm broke. Mary had declared she must have her Mass. As we might expect, her Guise uncles did the same. The whole of the queen's French retinue clamoured that 'They would to France without delay; that they could not live without the Mass'. John Knox's comment was 'And would to God that that menzie,[2] together with the Mass, had taken goodnight of this realm for ever'.[3] On Sunday, 24 August 1561 Mass was celebrated in the private chapel within the Palace. There was great excitement among the populace. 'The godly began to bolden; and men began to speak openly, "Shall that idol be suffered again to take place within this realm? It shall not."'. Lord James had heard the crowd muttering 'the idolater priest should die', and placed himself in the door of the chapel solemnly declaring that he was there to stop all Scots from entering in to the Mass. Lord John Stewart, commendator of Coldingham, and Lord Robert Stewart, commendator of Holyrood, both Protestants, saw to it that no harm was done to the priest. They were illegitimate sons of James V, and so half-brothers of both the queen and Lord James.

Next day, as there was danger of rioting, the Privy Council issued a proclamation in the queen's name forbidding anyone,

2.   menzie = company.

3.   John Knox, *History*, II, p. 9.

under pain of death, 'to take upon hand, privately or openly, to make alteration or innovation of the state of religion, or attempt anything against the form which her Majesty found publicly and universally standing at her Majesty's arrival in this her Realm.' At the same time severe penalties were threatened against any who should molest or trouble, in any way whatsoever, any of those who had come from France with her Grace.

The compromise was a weak one. It meant that the religion of the Court was to be Roman Catholicism and that of the nation Protestantism. It was contrary to the laws passed by Parliament only a year previously. Such an arrangement was fraught with grave danger. It could easily lead to open conflict, or, as was probably intended by the queen, it could be the first step towards the gradual ousting of Protestantism. It was a most unfortunate circumstance that at the time of the Reformation both sides – Protestants and Roman Catholics – cherished an erroneous conception of the unity of the Church inherited from medieval times. They both failed to realize fully that the unity of the Church proclaimed in the New Testament was a unity of the Spirit and not an outward, authoritative organization claiming to be the one and only Church of Christ in the world and insisting that they had the right to unchurch all who differed from them.

⟋⟋⟋

The Protestant Lords had clearly resolved upon a policy of compromise after the queen returned. Their motives may have been quite commendable but there was a lamentable failure to understand the grim realities of the situation. As one noble after another came to town to pay his respects to her Majesty, each, in turn, was horrified to know that the Mass was permitted. Each man, as he came, accused those that were before him, but 'after that they had remained a certain space, they were as quiet as were the former'. So much was this the case that a zealous and godly man, Robert Campbell of Kinzeancleuch, a steadfast friend of John Knox, said to Lord Ochiltree, 'My Lord, now ye are come, and almost the last of all the rest; and I perceive, by your anger, that the fire edge is not off you yet; but I fear that, after the holy water of the Court be sprinkled upon you, ye shall become as temperate as the rest ... I think there be some enchantment whereby men are bewitched.'[4] It is a clever description of what actually took place. The queen's ingratiating ways, her pleas for the rights of conscience, the subtle persuasions of Protestant supporters who claimed she could be won for their religion, blinded the minds of men and they resolved to suffer her policy.

While John Knox was eager not to offend men such as Lord James Stewart, whom he held in high esteem, and helped to slacken the excessive zeal of some violent opponents of the policy of the Court, he nevertheless attacked in the strongest possible terms the conduct of the queen and her retinue in hearing Mass. From his pulpit of St Giles', 'the best rostrum in the country', he declared that 'one Mass was more fearful unto him than if ten thousand armed enemies were landed in any part of the realm of purpose to suppress the whole religion.'[5] The obvious meaning of that 'one Mass' performed for the ruler 'who might soon have the power, and perhaps had already the intention, of suppressing religion', was a danger of the gravest kind.[6] The Palace sent for Knox, probably on the suggestion of Lord James who wished to bring together Queen Mary and the Reformer, for he liked and admired both in their

---

4.   John Knox, *History*, II, p. 12.

5.   John Knox, *op. cit.*, II, p. 12.

6.   Taylor Innes, *John Knox*, p. 122.

own way. The aim of her Majesty seems to have been to win over Knox to her side. The four famous interviews between them have been so widely publicized and discussed that we are not called upon now to do more than pick out the most salient points. The first interview at which Lord James was present was a veritable battle of wits showing great nimbleness of mind on both sides. Having taxed him with writing against women rulers (and so against her) in his *First Blast of the Trumpet*, and the matter having been fully discussed, she went on, 'But yet, ye have taught the people to receive another religion than their Princes allow: and how can that doctrine be of God, seeing that God commands subjects to obey their Princes?' Knox replied, 'Madam, as right religion took neither original nor authority from worldly princes, but from the Eternal God alone, so are not subjects bound to frame their religion according to the appetites of their Princes.' When the queen insisted that the biblical characters mentioned by Knox had not resisted their sovereigns with the sword, he replied that, if princes 'exceed their bounds' and go beyond their just limits 'they may be resisted even by power'. Knox agreed that it was within their 'bounds' to regulate the religion of their subjects as long as they did it aright and according to God's Word. Otherwise a prince who did evil might have to be restrained, like a father 'stricken with a frenzy'. The queen was amazed at what seemed to her with her absolutist ideas an astounding argument and remained in a daze 'more than a quarter of an hour'.

Recovering herself, she said, 'Well then, I perceive that my subjects shall obey you and not me.' 'God forbid,' replied the Reformer with conviction 'that ever I taken upon me to command any to obey me, or yet to set subjects at liberty to do what pleaseth them.' This was his genuine sentiment that men ought to honour 'kings and all who are in authority' (1 Tim. 2:2 NKJV).

When Knox declared that God 'commands queens to be nurses unto His people,' Mary answered, 'yea, but ye are not the Church that I will nourish: I will defend the Kirk of Rome, for, I think, it is the true Kirk of God.' This was certainly a strong and emphatic statement to be made by a queen whose counsellors were almost all Protestants and where Parliament had almost unanimously approved the doctrines of the Reformed faith.

The Reformer's reply was equally emphatic and far from showing any cringing spirit even in the presence of Majesty. 'Your will,' quoth he, 'Madam, is no reason; neither doth your thought make that Roman harlot to be the true and immaculate spouse of Jesus Christ.' Here is a declaration such as we might expect from one of the ancient Hebrew prophets delivering a stern oracle of God.

'My conscience,' said she, 'is not so.' 'Conscient, Madam,' answered Knox, 'requires knowledge, and I fear that right knowledge ye have none.'

The queen turned to the supposed difficulty of scriptural interpretation. 'Ye interpret the Scriptures,' said she, 'in one manner, and they interpret in another; whom shall I believe? And who shall be judge?' The Reformer's answer was ideal, 'Ye shall believe God, that plainly speaketh in His Word; and further than the Word teacheth you, ye shall neither believe the one nor the other. The Word of God is plain in itself; and if there appear any obscurity in one place, the Holy Ghost, who is never contrarious to Himself, explains the same more clearly in other places.'[7]

Although it must have been apparent to both the queen and Knox that their points of view were utterly irreconcilable, they parted with mutual courtesies. Outwardly, her Majesty

7.   See John Knox, *History*, II, pp. 13-20.

had remained friendly, and the Reformer had been loyal to his country. Immediately after the interview he expressed privately his assessment of her character: 'If there be not in her a proud mind, a crafty wit, and an indurate heart against God and His truth, my judgement faileth me.' They seem hard words and make no allowance, apparently, for the bad school of morals in which she had been reared, nor for her youth. Yet subsequent events conclusively proved that, on the whole, John Knox had come to a correct conclusion. He was almost the only man who did so at the time. Dr Donald MacMillan of Glasgow has sized up well the relative characters of the combatants: The queen represented the Hellenistic spirit and Knox the Hebraic. 'Mary was a child of nature, fond of pleasure, with no serious earnestness or strong feeling about religion. Knox, on the other hand, felt that he was acting not on his own responsibility, but as a servant of the Divine; that the truth committed to him must be held sacred at all hazards, and that not only was he bound to declare it on every occasion, but to resist to the death any who might dare to impugn it.'[8]

John Knox was no courtier. He was more like John the Baptist preaching his stern message of repentance than like a dweller in king's courts. Most people would agree with Randolph, the English envoy, when he wrote to Sir William Cecil about Knox, 'I commend better the success of his doings and preachings than the manner thereof.'[9] But there is no gainsaying the fact that he possessed a remarkable faculty for judging correctly the characters of the people he met as well as the implications of complicated situations. Again and again he was proved in the end to be correct when even his friends differed seriously from

---

8.   D. MacMillan, *John Knox*, p. 232.
9.   Randolph to Cecil, 24 October 1561.

him at the outset. In the interview with the queen just referred to he expressed views far ahead of his time and was declaring, in essence, that doctrine of limited monarchy under which our country has thrived so remarkably.

Queen Mary had not been long in Scotland before it became apparent that the Lords who had contended so valiantly for the Reformation when in opposition, were now prepared to compromise when basking in the smile of the sovereign. The queen not only had Mass in her private chapel, but people were asking, 'who can hinder any of her subjects from practising the queen's religion?' Mary was able to put the Provost and Bailies of Edinburgh in prison for enforcing the laws of 1560 against Roman Catholics. She also held great Popish celebrations in the palace on the night of All Saints and did not encounter opposition. Attempts were made by the nobles to place the Church under the authority of the crown and so destroy its freedom. Maitland of Lethington held that the General Assembly could not lawfully meet without the express sanction of the queen. To this John Knox pointedly replied, 'If the liberty of the Church should stand upon the queen's allowance or disallowance, we are assured not only to lack assemblies, but also to lack the public preachings of the evangel'. The affirmation was mocked by the courtiers, but Knox stood by his statement, declaring 'Time will try the truth'.[10]

The scornful attitude of the nobles to *The Book of Discipline* at the time of the December General Assembly in 1561 showed how well the 'holy water of the Court' had done its work. The sufferings of the ministers and readers, however, compelled the Privy Council to take some action for their relief. Since the Reformation they had received nothing from the revenues of the

10.   John Knox, *History*, II, p. 25.

old Church and were dependent on the haphazard benevolence of their congregations. Many were in a condition bordering on starvation. The Privy Council, composed of Protestant nobles, decided that two-thirds of the revenues from benefices should continue to be drawn by the old Roman Catholic incumbents. The remaining third of the revenue was assigned to the Crown for the payment of stipends to superintendents, ministers and readers. The claims of the Crown were first attended to, and then the preachers were given their share of the third. While these stipends were by no means excessive, they were fairly reasonable on paper. The grievous part of the business was that frequently they were not paid at all or were paid only in part, and this matter continued to be ground of complaint for many years. It is worth noting how generous was the treatment meted out by this Protestant Privy Council to the former Roman Catholic holders of benefices. It must be almost without precedent. The bishops, abbots, priors and others in the higher ecclesiastical ranks were left in comfort for life, but among the lower grades there were not a few cases of dreadful poverty. As the old Roman Catholic incumbents died out, the revenues they had enjoyed were taken possession of by one or another of the greedy nobles who were always looking for more. The small provision made for the Church was denounced by John Knox as iniquitous,[11] for he had always taken the view that the patrimony of the Kirk should be allocated in its entirety to the Church. His conception was that the Church should be made trustee for the administration of all these endowments, one third being for the maintenance of the ministry and the remainder exclusively for education and the poor.

---

11.   John Knox, *op. cit.*, II, p. 29.

13

THE POLICY OF COMPROMISE

Certain Protestant courtiers were prepared to compromise with Mary, especially Lord James Stewart and Lethington. The latter was a humanist and man of the world. He had no deep religious principles, and compromise came easy to him. Lord James was very different. He was 'the man whom all the godly did most reverence,' but he honestly believed that if the queen were given some latitude in religious matters she could be won for the Reformed Church. She played her game very skilfully, being even prepared to take stern measures against men of her own faith as long as she depended on the Protestant nobles. Thus, with Lord James, she fought and defeated the very powerful Roman Catholic noble, the Earl of Huntly. Her action in regard to Parliament in 1563 is still more illuminating. She had called no session of the Estates since her return from France. The matter could be no longer postponed. Knox and the General Assembly were insistently pressing for the ratification of *The Book of Discipline*. The nobles strongly opposed ratification, for, by so doing, they would condemn themselves for taking possession of the patrimony of the Kirk. The queen was against ratification because it would greatly strengthen the position of the Reformed Church. She and the nobles knew that, if the lesser barons and burgh representatives attended in such numbers as in 1560, they would probably insist on *The Book of Discipline* being adopted. How could it be prevented?

The nobles argued that the Church must wait until the queen asked Parliament for favours and then press the matter. Her Majesty played a master stroke. She began prosecuting even eminent Roman Catholics for hearing Mass. The Protestants believed she was now coming over to their side and were lulled to sleep. They felt the policy of the General Assembly would be carried in Parliament without question. The best Protestants did not attend, and nothing was done about adopting *The Book of Discipline*.

John Knox blamed his old friend Lord James Stewart (now Earl of Moray). Feeling ran so high that 'familiarly after that time they spoke not together more than a year and a half.'[1] The Reformer was virtually abandoned by his old friends, the former Lords of the Congregation, and for two years they could scarcely be persuaded to attend meetings of the General Assembly, which was solidly behind him. This ageing man, however, although scorned by the mightiest in the land, stood steadfast against every wind that blew. The first Lord's Day after Parliament rejected *The Book of Discipline*, Knox presented his case to the nation from the pulpit of St Giles in the presence of most of the nobility. He reminded them of God's mercies in past days. 'In your most extreme dangers I have been with you. St Johnstone, Cupar Muir and the Craigs of Edinburgh are yet recent in my heart; yea that dark and dolorous night wherein all ye, my Lords, with shame and fear left this town, is yet in my mind, and God forbid that ever I forget it.' He appealed to them not to betray God's cause when they had it in their hands to establish it as they pleased. Let them ask of the queen that

1.   John Knox, *History*, II, pp. 78, 79.

which by God's Word they might justly require. Let them not resile from their 'former stoutness in God'.

John Knox ended the sermon with a reference to the reports circulating about the queen's forthcoming marriage. 'Dukes, brethren to Emperors, and Kings, strive all for the best game ... but whensoever the Nobility of Scotland professing the Lord Jesus, consents that an infidel (and all papists are infidels) shall be head to your Sovereign, ye do so far as in ye lieth to banish Christ Jesus from the Realm.' Immediately flatterers carried a report of the sermon to the Palace and the Reformer was at once summoned into the royal presence for the fourth and last time. On the third occasion, at Loch Leven, the interview had ended most happily. It is probable that Her Majesty had enjoyed her previous dialectical battles with the Reformer. The present situation was different. The reference to her marriage stung her to the quick. She still had her heart set on marrying Don Carlos, the heir of Philip II of Spain, a man full of bigotry. But she knew that Knox had a strong case. Immediately he entered she burst into tears. 'The queen,' says Knox, 'in a vehement fume, began to cry out that never prince was handled as she was. "I have," said she, "borne with you in all your rigorous manner of speaking ... and yet I cannot be quit of you. I vow to God I shall be revenged."'

As soon as he could say a word, Knox began to explain how in 'the preaching place' he was not master of himself, but must obey God who commanded him 'to speak plainly, and to flatter no flesh upon the face of the earth.' 'But what have you to do,' said she, 'with my marriage?' The Reformer was proceeding to explain how he must preach repentance and faith when he was brought back sharply to the point. 'What have you to do with my marriage? Or what are you in this commonwealth?' Knox's reply has become famous: 'A subject born within the same,

165

Madam. And albeit I am neither earl, lord, nor baron within it, yet has God made me – how abject that ever I am in your eyes – a profitable member within the same.' He then repeated to his sovereign the deadly consequences to her country if the nobility ever consented to her being 'subject to an unfaithful husband'. The argument was unanswerable. Mary could only burst into a flood of tears. When Knox tried clumsily to console her it offended her still more, and she ordered him to depart and await her pleasure in the ante-room. There he found himself shunned of all. He 'stood in the chamber, as one whom men had never seen (so were all afraid), except that Lord Ochiltree bore him company'. Finally, he was allowed to go home.[2]

In regard to John Knox's interviews with Queen Mary, the words of Dr Donald MacMillan of Glasgow are worth considering:

It should be remembered that he only conversed with her when she sent for him, and that he had to defend himself, always single-handed, against charges, some of them of the most serious nature. His speech had to be plain and strong, and we must admit that his words are sufficiently civil. It was really the queen who tried to browbeat him and not he the queen. Mary Stewart would have shown much more respect for herself if, after the first interview with Knox, she had left him alone ... In summoning him so often to her presence, and in revealing in the discussions much that was womanly weak and unwomanly violent, she did herself a disservice, both at the time and in the eyes of posterity.[3]

The question naturally arises why John Knox, who was not without kindness and good humour, should so consistently and relentlessly have opposed the queen. It was because he knew

2.   John Knox, *History*, II, pp. 82-4.

3.   Dr Donald MacMillan, *John Knox*, pp. 269, 270.

what few of her subjects would believe – that her constant aim from the first day of her return to Scotland was to lead her country back into the Roman fold. She gave innumerable promises that she would never alter the religion of her people, and yet all the time she was engaged in crafty intrigues to destroy the Protestant faith. Very few could credit it, but Knox knew it, although only in part. Look at a few of the facts.

Nicolas de Gouda, a Jesuit, was sent in the summer of 1562 as Nuncio to Scotland by Pope Pius IV, to initiate through Queen Mary means and methods to re-establish the Roman faith in her kingdom. He was charged to secure a strong base for future action. The queen cunningly arranged to have a secret meeting with him at the exact hour on 24 July 1562 when her Protestant entourage were attending their own religious services. She knew well that her people regarded de Gouda's mission as a danger to the country and yet she received him secretly.[4]

De Gouda read to her the Pope's brief, and he himself wrote a narrative of her reply.

> She hoped the supreme Pontiff would have regard to her ready will rather than to anything she had actually done since her return ... She herself, and the other adherents of the orthodox religion, had been obliged to do many things which they did not like, in order to preserve the last traces of the Catholic faith and worship in the country .... For herself, she would rather forfeit her life than abandon her faith.[5]

In keeping with this, she wrote on 31 January 1563 to Pope Pius IV: 'It being ever our intention, since our return to this kingdom, to employ, as we have done, our studies, thoughts,

---

4.   Donald Maclean, *Counter-Reformation*, pp. 26-30 and D. Hay Fleming, *Mary Queen of Scots*, p. 268.

5   Father Pollen, *Papal Negotiations*, pp. 130-9.

labour and manners, such as it has pleased God to give us, in bringing back to the truth our poor subjects, whom we have with the greatest displeasure found to have wandered from the good path, and to be plunged in the new opinions and damnable errors, which are now prevalent in many places of Christendom.' She went on to express the hope that all her subjects would yet 'worthily acknowledge the holy Roman Catholic Church, in the obedience of which we wish to live your most devoted daughter. To which end we shall spare no effort in our power, even life itself, if need be.'[6]

Six weeks later she wrote to the Council of Trent lamenting her inability to send representatives to that Synod and commissioning her uncle, the Cardinal of Lorraine, to explain her helplessness. The letter was received with great delight in a special secret session. 'The Queen's letter, and the Cardinal's speech, were received with every mark of respect; and the Synod by the mouth of its prolocutor, declared its conviction that the name of Mary of Scotland would be had in everlasting remembrance as the name of a sovereign prepared to suffer the loss of all, even of life itself, for the faith.'[7] Let it be carefully observed that the letter to the Council of Trent was written only two months before she made her plans for prosecuting forty-eight Roman Catholics for celebrating Mass, and most of them were sent to ward. One wonders just how much they really suffered by their incarceration, but by such doings she was able to cast dust into the eyes of her nobles.

It is amazing to see how Mary could speak so easily with two voices. For example, in May 1565, in view of her forthcoming

---

6. D. Hay Fleming, *Mary Queen of Scots*, p. 269. Quoting Turnbull's *Mary's Letters* (1845) pp. 142, 143 and Labanoff's *Recueil*, I, pp. 177, 178.

7. D. Hay Fleming, *op. cit.*, p. 269. Quoting Labanoff's *Recueil*, I, pp. 177, 178; and Robertson's *Statuta*, I, pp. 166, 167.

marriage with Darnley,[8] the queen gave ample promises to the Lords that their religion would be securely established.[9] About the same time she and Darnley promised the pope 'that they would defend the Catholic religion to the utmost of their power.'[10] In a matter of seven weeks, at the time of her marriage, she issued four proclamations assuring her subjects that the Protestant religion would not be molested. Three weeks later she wrote to Philip II of Spain imploring his aid in averting the ruin of the Catholic religion in her kingdom, and in frustrating the establishment of the unhappy errors which she and her husband were resisting 'to the hazard of their crown.' Within a week she made a Proclamation that Parliament would be convened so that all acts and laws prejudicial to the Reformed religion of Scotland should be abolished. The Parliament, however, was abruptly dissolved, and she wrote to her ambassador in France – Archbishop James Beaton – that at its opening one important step had been taken 'tending to have done some good anent restoring the auld religion.'[11]

Not only was Mary very much under the influence of her Guise uncles, especially the Duke of Guise and the Cardinal of Lorraine, she was also in very close touch with Philip II of Spain, the most powerful and the most bigoted monarch in Europe. Even when the plans for a Spanish match miscarried through the secret intervention of Mary's enemy, Catherine de Medici, the French Queen Mother, this Spanish influence continued to perturb the peace of Scotland and England. Gueran de Spes,

---

8.   See pp. 177, 178 regarding the marriage.

9.   David Calderwood, *History*, II, p. 570.

10. Robertson's *Statuta*, I, p. 169.

11. See D. Hay Fleming, *Mary Queen of Scots*, pp. 122, 123, where all is thoroughly documented. This Archbishop Beaton was a nephew of Cardinal David Beaton and was formerly Archbishop of Glasgow.

the Spanish ambassador, wrote to Philip in 1568 that the time was favourable for intervention in Scotland to restore Mary to the throne[12] and 'for restoring the country to the Catholic religion.' All along, the aim of Spain was to dethrone Queen Elizabeth and place Mary upon the throne of England. Dr Donald Maclean of Edinburgh, in writing about the dangers facing Britain at this time from the House of Guise on one hand, and from Philip II on the other, says:

> That there was real danger to the realm from Roman Catholic aspirations is clearly proved by such unmistakable signs and events as the excommunication of Queen Elizabeth in 1570, and the intrigues for her assassination to secure a Roman Catholic successor, the massacre of St Bartholomew's Eve, brutally effected by the Guise, which received the fervid and cordial approval of the Pope, and the plotting of the Scottish Roman Catholic nobleman Lord Seton, and others, with the Duke of Alva to invade Scotland.[13]

Philip II had indeed given instructions in 1568 to his commander-in-chief, the Duke of Alva, to do his utmost to aid the proposed rebellion in Scotland in favour of the dethroned Queen Mary.

When we consider all these facts we begin to realize that John Knox, after all, had solid grounds for his stern opposition to the queen. The times were dangerous. Treachery abounded. A strong man was required in that hour of need. No man has ever had a stronger sense of duty than John Knox, and no man has ever carried out his duty more steadfastly, even when standing alone in the face of dislike and obloquy. He

---

12. For the events leading up to her abdication in 1567 see chapter 14 pp. 188-91.

13. Donald Maclean, *Counter-Reformation in Scotland,* pp. 37, 38.

had opposed strenuously the policy of compromise followed from 1561 to 1565 by the Earl of Moray, Lethington and the other courtiers. Strangely enough Vincenzo Laureo, Bishop of Mondovi, who was sent by the pope as Nuncio to Scotland in 1566 urged Mary to put to death 'the six miscreants'. These were the Earl of Moray (Lord James Stewart), Argyll, Morton, Lethington, Bellenden and a commoner called McGill, the very men who had been most closely connected with the policy of conciliation. De Gouda in 1562 had brought a similar request from Pope Pius IV who urged Mary 'to follow the example of Queen Mary of England, now departed in Christ'. As we have had the unpleasant task of recording much against the Scottish queen, it is gratifying to be able to record, to her very great credit, that on both occasions she indignantly refused, declaring that she would not imbrue her hands in the blood of her subjects. The fact that such suggestions could have been made reveals what a violent and lawless age it was and that only a strong, heroic man of the stamp of Knox could have availed to save the Reformation from destruction in Scotland.

One of the most dramatic episodes in the life of Knox was when the Queen had him summoned before the Council toward the end of 1563 and charged with treason. He was accused of 'convocating the lieges' because he had sent out a circular letter at the request of the Church asking them to attend in Edinburgh to secure justice for two Protestants who were on trial on a charge of riotous behaviour. It was a most serious occasion. Knox had no-one in the Council to support him. If they voted against him, his life would be in jeopardy. The Earl of Moray and Lethington tried to persuade him to confess his guilt and cast himself on the queen's mercy. He absolutely refused. Lethington then tried to catch him with subterfuges, but found the Reformer could not be so easily deceived. The trial then proceeded. Mary felt that at last she had Knox in her power. In her elation she forgot her queenly dignity. 'When she saw John Knox standing at the other end of the table, bareheaded, she first smiled and after gave a gauff of laughter, whereat placebos[14] gave their plaudit.' Then, speaking in excellent Scots, she said, 'But wot ye whereat I laugh? Yon man made me greet[15] and grat never a tear himself. I will see if I can gar[16] him greet.' Knox acknowledged he had written the letter and declined a request from the Council to withdraw it. In reply to the charges read out by Lethington, he gave an able disquisition on lawful and unlawful assemblies, which impressed the Council. When he proceeded to show the danger of allowing the Roman Church to gain the ascendancy again, he was interrupted, probably by Lethington, with the words, 'You forget you are not now in the pulpit.' Promptly came the historic reply, 'I am in the place where I am demanded by conscience to speak the truth, and therefore the truth I speak, impugn it whoso list.'

As Knox developed his theme it became apparent to all, Protestants and Catholics, that he was right. They saw that if meetings could only be held with the queen's consent the whole nation would be placed in peril. Even men like Bishop Sinclair and Lord Ruthven, a fervent adherent of Mary's, were forced to concede this. The Council unanimously acquitted John Knox. Her Majesty was indignant and ordered the vote to be taken a second time, but the nobles were adamant and the result was the same. The queen's chagrin was very great. Knox knew this and added a sly reference in his *History*, 'That night was neither dancing nor fiddling in the Court, for Madam was disappointed of her purpose, which was to have had John Knox in her will by vote of her nobility.'

---

14. placeboes = 'yes-men'.

15. greet = weep.

16. gar = compel.

⟡

Notwithstanding this favourable vote, the Protestant courtiers continued to look askance at the General Assembly during the whole of 1564. In a conference held to foster better relations between them, Lethington demanded, 'Then will ye make subjects to control their princes and rulers?' Knox gave one of his famous replies: 'And what harm should the Commonwealth receive, if that the corrupt affections of ignorant rulers were moderated, and so bridled by the wisdom and discretion of godly subjects that they should do wrong nor violence to no man?' Outside of the great dictatorships everyone accepts this doctrine nowadays; but in Queen Mary's time the idea of a ruler governing by consent of a Council seemed utterly outrageous.

In spite of Knox's unpopularity with the courtiers in 1564 there are remarkable indications as to his power and influence. Thus, he was sought out in his house by the Earl of Bothwell who afterwards married Queen Mary. The Earl was well entertained and received a promise that Knox would use his influence with the Earl of Arran to bring to an end an old feud, and this the Reformer was able to do with happy results. On a certain Sunday evening the Duke of Chatelherault, once Governor of Scotland, and Randolph, the English Ambassador, are found with Knox at supper discussing the national situation and the future of Protestantism. Such events reveal that Knox's influence continued great not only with the commonalty but with the nobles outside the court circle as well.

It was in this year, 1564, that our Reformer astonished the nation and married a second time at the age of 59[17] to

---

17.   The question of the date of Knox's birth has not been satisfactorily settled. Until 1905 most historians believed he was born in 1505. Early in the twentieth century Dr Hay Fleming and other distinguished writers began to place the date between 1513 and 1515. It seems an insuperable objection to this that all accounts of Knox, in his latter years, concur in describing him as a very frail old man (cf. James Melville, *Diary*, p. 33). These descriptions of him would be inappropriate to a man of 55 or 56. We adhere to the traditional date of 1505.

Margaret Stewart, the seventeen-year-old daughter of Lord Ochiltree. The queen was very indignant at this marriage, not because of the disparity in age but because Margaret Stewart was of royal 'blood' and distantly related to herself.

Margaret proved a good and faithful wife to Knox. They had three daughters, and at least one of these proved a valiant defender of the Presbyterian cause when, as the wife of the Rev. John Welch, she had to enter into a disputation with King James VI. It is an interesting fact that in the Ochiltree family John Knox was regarded as being quite as good a match for Margaret as a great noble would have been.

The year 1564 must have been a testing one for the Reformer for he found himself alienated from most of the nobility who attended at court. Old friends like the Earls of Argyll, Moray, Morton and Rothes received him coldly because he disapproved of their temporizing policy with the queen. They were even very suspicious of the General Assembly for, as we have noted already, it was staunchly loyal to John Knox, and they only countenanced it grudgingly.

By the end of the year, however, these, together with the other Protestant courtiers, began to be uneasy as to Mary's plans. They were kept in the dark as to her aims and found they could not be responsible for her actions. Her confidential secretary, David Rizzio, an Italian, was becoming more and more influential in her counsels, and she was daily becoming more independent of her courtiers and even of her old friends in France. It finally became evident that matters were hastening to a crisis, for the land was now openly subjected to absolute government. The queen would not brook any opposition to her plans.

14

WAS JOHN KNOX RIGHT?

Early in 1565 it became clear that the queen was preparing to pursue a more public and more aggressive policy in favour of the Roman Church. Philip II of Spain had changed his mind several times on the question of the proposed marriage of his son Don Carlos to Mary. This was clearly the match on which she herself had set her heart. It was now apparent that this Spanish marriage, which would have raised her to the most powerful throne in the world, was not to take place. At the same time, however, at least a dozen others from the highest ruling circles in Europe were eagerly soliciting her hand. Unfortunately, Queen Elizabeth of England did not prove helpful when consulted on these important questions. She was obviously jealous of the beautiful Scottish queen who was the heir to her throne, but whose claim she would never acknowledge, partly because Mary had never acknowledged Elizabeth's own right to be queen of England.

At this time there was a decided drawing together of the Catholic powers with the intention of finally crushing Protestant heresy. The rivalry between France and Spain was being overcome so that under papal guidance they could join in this crusade. Even in England there was considerable danger to Elizabeth's throne from the disaffection of powerful Roman

Catholic nobles who would gladly have joined a movement to give Mary of Scotland the crown, and they were being strongly encouraged from abroad, especially by Philip II of Spain. 'Philip had one single object before him – the Church, of which he had become the sworn champion. For the Church, but for the Church alone, and for nothing else in this world, he was prepared to plunder and torture and forswear himself, to do anything required.'[1]

Whatever her own personal feelings may have been, the closest ties of Queen Mary on the continent were with people of this type. The ruthless Duke of Alva, early in 1565, disclosed in a letter to Philip that at the request of her uncle, the Cardinal of Lorraine, he had given audience to an envoy from the Queen of Scots. The envoy told him there would certainly be a revolution in England, and he desired to know what course his mistress should take. He gave the advice that Mary should 'meanwhile conduct herself not only with reserve, but dissimulation towards Elizabeth. If she conducted herself to the satisfaction of the king of Spain, he would bring to her such aid, at the time when it was least expected, that she would certainly accomplish her object'.[2] It was a time when many Protestants in Europe were in deadly peril.

~~~

The rise to power of David Rizzio in Scotland was symptomatic of the queen's new policy. He had come to Scotland as a musician in the service of the ambassador of Piedmont, and quickly secured a remarkable ascendancy over Her Majesty. On 3 June 1565 Randolph, the English ambassador, wrote to Leicester that Rizzio's pride was intolerable and his words not

1.   J. Hill Burton, *History of Scotland*, IV, p. 133.

2.   *Ibid.*.

to be borne. It was widely believed that he was a secret agent of the pope. Whether he was or not, he considered it his duty to further in every way the interests of the Roman Church; and it was he who had charge of the queen's correspondence with the Catholic powers on the continent. It was largely through his influence that the predominantly Protestant Council, of which the Earl of Moray and Lethington were members, was brought down.

After twenty years of exile in England, the Earl of Lennox was allowed to return to Scotland in the autumn of 1564. In February, his son Henry, Lord Darnley, joined him. They belonged to the Stewart family, like the Queen of Scotland, and Darnley was next in succession to the English throne after Mary herself. They were both great-grandchildren of Henry VII. As soon as the queen met Lord Darnley she became infatuated with this handsome young cousin. His good looks, at this stage, seem to have been his only attractive quality. Rizzio did all he could to promote the match, for Darnley was a Roman Catholic, and he had also private reasons for favouring his suit. Early in April 1565 they were either betrothed or secretly married in Rizzio's apartment in the Palace. No-one knew of this at the time, and reason for the secrecy is unknown. On 29 June of that year they were publicly married in the Chapel Royal of Holyrood House by John Sinclair, Dean of Restalrig. Mary ordered that her husband be given the title of king. 'During the space of three or four days, there was nothing but balling, and dancing, and banqueting.'[3]

The situation in the nation, however, was far from happy. One of the first public actions of the queen and Darnley was to send out orders to raise men for the army by beat of tabor and

---

3.   John Knox, *History*, II, p. 158.

drums. After the rise of Rizzio to power, the Earl of Moray, till then the most influential person in the country after the sovereign, became very cool and eventually bitterly hostile in his attitude to Her Majesty. In the opinion of John Knox, the root cause of the trouble was the religious question; others thought it was envy on Moray's part because of the exaltation of Darnley and Rizzio. Randolph wrote to Cecil on 13 October mentioning a grave rumour as to her conduct with Rizzio. Such reports were widespread but all we can say is that Mary must be given the benefit of the doubt.

Almost immediately after the queen's marriage the more earnest of the Protestant lords withdrew from Edinburgh and moved to the west. They were declared rebels by the queen and her husband. About 15 August they met at Ayr and made arrangements for their defence. Among them were the Duke of Chatelherault, the Earls of Moray, Argyll, Glencairn, Rothes, and the Lords Boyd and Ochiltree, with various other Barons and Gentlemen of Fife and Ayrshire. These Lords had bound themselves together by a bond of mutual defence. During the whole of the earlier part of the year Mary and Rizzio ruled with absolute power. The Roman Catholic party became very much stronger and bolder, and were now holding services openly in many parts. Even so, the queen pretended to be more than usually interested in the Reformed Church and actually toyed with the idea of going to hear the Protestant preachers, especially Erskine of Dun whom she liked because he was 'a mild and sweet-natured man, with true honesty and uprightness'. When, however, the General Assembly of June 1565 brought matters to an issue she showed herself inflexibly Roman Catholic and refused to break with the Catholic powers whose hostile designs towards the Protestant cause were by then apparent to all.

Knox and the Earl of Moray had been completely reconciled by this time, but even their combined efforts could not stem the rising tide of opposition. While Knox had strong support among the commonalty of Edinburgh, the Reformed Church had at this time no friend at court. But the fact that Mary's cause was so strong and that the Protestant nobles were in the west and declared to be rebels, did not daunt Knox who went on preaching in St Giles'. On 19 August, Darnley attended the service. He had the misfortune to hear a thundering sermon on Isaiah 26:13: 'O Lord our God, other lords than thou have ruled over us'. It was clearly aimed at the queen and himself. Darnley was so furious that when he returned to the palace he could not dine, and in his evil temper 'he passed in the afternoon to his hawking.'[4] Possibly the fresh air soothed him. That very night Knox was summoned from his bed to appear before the Privy Council composed of the Earl of Atholl, Lord Ruthven, and three high legal functionaries of the court. He was suspended from preaching in Edinburgh while the king and queen remained in the city. John Craig was to supply his place meanwhile in St Giles'. The Edinburgh City Council however, strongly and unanimously supported him.

In about a week's time, Mary put herself at the head of her army and with incredible vigour marched from town to town and from county to county, keeping the tiny army of the Protestant nobles in constant flight. During this conflict, known as the Round-about-Raid, the Protestants were outnumbered by four to one by Mary's forces. Finally the leaders took refuge in England where they sought the help and sympathy of Queen

---

4.   John Knox, *History*, II, p. 159.

Elizabeth. Whatever may be said of Queen Mary, she can never be accused of lack of courage. On this occasion she rode before her troops 'in a steel cap with pistols at her saddlebow'.

In the north of England, the Scottish Protestant nobles were well received by the Earl of Bedford who was entirely in sympathy with them. Queen Elizabeth gave a very cold, if not hostile, reception to the Scottish 'rebels'. When the Earl of Moray and the Commendator of Kilwinning went to London to seek her help, she scolded them sternly for their audacity. In the presence of the French and Spanish ambassadors, she charged them with being rebels and traitors to their legitimate sovereign, and expressed her indignation at their coming to her who was herself a sovereign. Elizabeth had almost a phobia in regard to subjects rebelling against their sovereign no matter how unjust or tyrannical he might be.

At this time, the cause of Protestantism in Scotland was in an exceedingly precarious condition. The policy of compromise favoured for four years by Moray, Lethington and the other Protestant courtiers had now proved a complete failure. It had enabled Mary to strengthen greatly her own position and that of the Roman Church in Scotland. Knox had warned them incessantly, but they merely scoffed at his warnings and despised his prophecies of coming evil. Events proved that he had far more political foresight and understanding than they. Never has any man been thoroughly vindicated than was John Knox in the Proclamation issued at Dumfries by the defeated Protestant nobles in 1565 before crossing over into England. When the General Assembly met in Edinburgh in December 1565 it was attended by, among other nobles, the Earls of Morton and Mar, Lord Lindsay and Secretary Lethington. The

Assembly resolved to appoint a National Fast to supplicate the mercy of God in the dark days through which they were passing.

It was currently believed that the queen's sharpness towards Protestants at this time was largely due to the sinister influence of David Rizzio, who enjoyed favour in the palace to a degree which many considered unseemly. He had made himself intolerable by his arrogance. Darnley had now become extremely jealous of him. The queen's marriage, which at first seemed so happy, soon became a source of misery and bitterness.

> The wife had great genius and sagacity; the husband was a fool, and a vicious and presumptuous fool. There is scarcely to be found his character the vestige of a good quality. The resources of his power and rank seem to have been considered by him only as elements of animal enjoyment, and of a vain-glorious assumption of superiority.[5]

Meanwhile the queen and her advisers had made arrangements to have the banished lords attainted, and a Bill of Attainder was prepared to be dealt with on 12 March 1566. This was dramatically prevented by the action of Lord Darnley who, filled with mad jealousy and deeply offended because the queen would not give him the crown matrimonial, sought out some of the discontented Lords who still remained in Scotland and entered into a compact with them to murder David Rizzio. Besides Darnley, there were involved in this conspiracy the Earl of Morton, the Master of Ruthven and others. On 9 March 1566 Darnley entered the Queen's Cabinet, where she was at supper with her half-sister, the Countess of Argyll, and David Rizzio. The nobles concerned in the plot then entered. The queen tried to protect her favourite, but he was dragged violently

---

5.   J. Hill Burton, *History of Scotland*, IV, p. 137.

into another room and despatched by the conspirators with many dagger wounds, Darnley insisting that his dagger be left sticking in Rizzio's body as a sign of his hatred. When Mary was told that he was dead she wiped away her tears, saying, 'No more tears, I will think upon revenge.'

Next day, the king issued a Proclamation dissolving the Parliament which was to have outlawed Moray and the other banished lords and to have confiscated their possessions. It ordered all who had come to the capital for the parliamentary session to leave town. That evening Moray and his supporters returned to Scotland and conferences were entered into with the queen to secure their pardon. With much craft she brought over Darnley to her side and with sweet words detached him from his fellow conspirators. Very basely he laid all the blame on the others and revealed their identity and protested his own innocence. She pretended to accept his explanations. The Earl of Morton acting on behalf of the assassins had brought a body of men and secured control of the palace. Having posted his armed forces, he sent home Bothwell and Huntly who were strong supporters of Her Majesty. Mary and Darnley escaped from Holyrood by stealth two days later, before dawn, and rode to Dunbar. There the queen's friends gathered around her. Soon they marched on Edinburgh with 8,000 men and the conspirators fled to save their lives. As Darnley had so treacherously betrayed them, they took their revenge by producing, for the queen's inspection, the documents which had been signed and sealed by him as leader of the conspiracy, and which also openly asserted the dishonour of his wife.

Mary continued for a time to use her husband to suit her own policy, but she despised him in her heart and never really forgave him for this grave insult. From this time onwards Darnley became more and more an object of contempt among the nobles, in spite of occasions when the queen seemed, at least outwardly, to show him a measure of affection. As time went on, the coolness developed into virtual hatred and the relations of the queen and her husband provided a theme for scandalmongers, not only in Scotland but in every court in Europe.

On her return to Edinburgh after the murder of Rizzio, Mary found herself more powerful than ever. She was surrounded mostly by the Catholic party and a few nominally Protestant nobles. The description given by Knox of those who supported Mary in this new phase of her history is worth recalling for the light it casts upon the development of events, and also as a sample of the Reformer's piquant style:

> The head is known: the tail has two branches; the temporal Lords that maintain her abominations, and her flattering councillors, blasphemous Balfour, now called Clerk of Register, Sinclair, Dean of Restalrig and Bishop of Brechin, blind of one eye in the body, but of both in his soul, upon whom God shortly took vengeance; John Lesley, priest's gett,[6] Abbot of Lindores and Bishop of Ross, Simon Preston of Craigmillar, a right epicurean, whose end it will be, or it be long, according to their works.[7]

For the time being the Catholic party was again in the ascendant and the Reformed Church lacked the support of those in high places. On 17 March 1566 John Knox, too, departed for the west which caused 'a great mourning of the godly of religion' in Edinburgh. At last we see the Reformer in a really dejected frame of spirit. On 12 March he wrote his famous confession

6.   Priest's gett = priest's child.

7.   John Knox, *History*, I, pp. 112, 113.

beginning, 'Be merciful unto me, O Lord, and call not into judgement my manifold sins; and chiefly those whereof the world is not able to accuse me.' He had prefaced this confession with the prayer, 'Lord Jesus receive my spirit, and put an end at Thy good pleasure to this my miserable life, for justice and truth are not to be found among the children of men.' The tremendous struggle in which he had been the leading figure was now telling on mind and body. Like the great prophet Elijah under the juniper tree who, in a terrible mental reaction, prayed that he might die, John Knox at this time was taking 'goodnight at the world and at all the fasherie[8] of the same', to quote his own words. Fortunately this depression was destined to pass away and to be replaced once again by his characteristic buoyant confidence.

When she was at Dunbar in March 1566, the queen had called to her aid the Earl of Bothwell. He has been frequently described as a noble of the swash-buckler kind, rash and venturesome. He was the last man who should have been called upon to guide Scottish affairs at such a time. Mary was destined to fall more and more under his influence and this was soon to prove her undoing.

The queen began to realize that her aggressive Roman Catholic policy had gone too far. Little by little during 1566 she relaxed and allowed one after another the banished lords to return. She even began to manifest more generous sentiments towards the Protestant Church. The hand of Bothwell may be seen in this. The General Assembly, however, was greatly alarmed when on 23 December John Hamilton, Archbishop of St Andrews, was restored to full Consistorial Jurisdiction contrary to the laws of 1560. John Knox, who by then had returned to Edinburgh and had taken a leading part in the

---

8.   fasherie = troubles.

Assembly, was asked to endeavour to stir up the nobles to a sense of the possible danger to the Protestant cause.

After the General Assembly, Knox set out for England to visit his two sons by his first marriage, as well as to renew old friendships in the sphere where he had laboured. At that time some of the more puritanical ministers in the Church of England were being deprived of their benefices because they refused to use 'surplice, corner-cap, and tippet'. At the request of the General Assembly, John Knox had addressed a letter to the pastors and bishops of that Church beseeching them to deal tenderly with the consciences of their brethren. It may safely be assumed that while in England the Reformer would do his utmost to strengthen the hands of those in the Anglican Church who were striving to maintain a robust Protestant witness on the lines of the Reformed Church on the continent. It is also not unlikely that, as opportunity arose, he would endeavour to interest those in high places in the struggle that was being waged by the Church in Scotland against hostile forces in that country.

The criticism has been levelled against Knox that, instead of going to England, he ought to have been using all his energy to resist the restoration of Archbishop Hamilton in Scotland, and that his absence then might make him seem indirectly responsible for Bothwell's rise to power. The accusation is groundless. John Knox had long intended to visit his sons in England where they were being brought up by their mother's relatives. He went with the cordial approval of the General Assembly which formally granted him leave of absence and provided him with letters of recommendation to various parties in England. They would not have done so had they considered that the Scottish Church, or people, would suffer injury through his absence.

—*—

Bothwell had become Her Majesty's favourite at least nine months before this and she speedily gave him a foremost place in the realm. He 'had now, of all men, greatest access and familiarity with the queen, so that nothing of any great importance was done without him.'[9] Far from this making the position of the Church more difficult, it eased the situation appreciably. As a result, not only did Her Majesty allow Knox to return to Edinburgh after an absence of some months in the west and in Fife, but she also showed herself anxious to secure the goodwill of the Protestants and signed an offer for a considerable sum for the better maintenance of the ministers, and this offer came before the General Assembly. Bothwell, while far from being a man of exemplary life, was nevertheless nominally a Protestant, and this had some effect upon the queen. Indeed, from that point of view, it seemed quite an opportune time for John Knox to leave Scotland for a short period. It is true that the raising of Archbishop Hamilton to Consistorial Jurisdiction caused some consternation in the Church, and the Assembly entered its protest and asked John Knox to warn the people of danger from popish aggression. At the same time, everyone knew that Hamilton counted for little in Scottish affairs then, whether in Church or State, and the possibility of his ever again exercising real power must have seemed a remote one. Knox might well set out on his much-needed and well-earned holiday without undue worry about the discredited Archbishop. The one and only reason for the elevation of the latter was revealed, a few months later, at the time of the murder of Darnley, when he annulled the marriage of Bothwell with Lady Jane Gordon which had only taken place on 24 February 1566. It was in

9.   John Knox, *History*, II, p. 184.

order to prepare the way for Bothwell's marriage with the queen, and this was the only ecclesiastical function ever discharged by Hamilton after his reinstatement, and almost certainly the only one he was expected to fulfil.

***

Meanwhile an event of very great import took place in Scotland – the murder of Lord Darnley. On 19 June 1566 a son had been born to him and to the queen in Edinburgh Castle. This was James VI who was destined to unite the crowns of England and Scotland in 1603. One of the factors which had attracted Mary to Darnley was that, after herself, he was the next heir to the throne of England. She must have felt that their union would make their claim to succession to the English throne almost irresistible. As Darnley was a Catholic, like herself, and they had strong support on the continent, she doubtless dreamt of bringing back not only Scotland, but also England to the Roman fold. There is pathos in the fact that when their child, of whom they expected so much, was baptized at Stirling on 17 December 1566 with all the rites of the Roman Church and with the greatest splendour and pomp which that Church could then muster in Scotland, Darnley was not present, although he was living in the town at the time. Neither was he present at any of the ceremonies which were celebrated after the baptism, a clear indication of the strained relations between husband and wife. On the other hand, Bothwell was given a leading place and the arrangements for the occasion were in his hands. According to the *Book of Articles*, Darnley had been humiliated and ignored, and stinted in his necessary expenses. He set out for Glasgow and almost immediately he was seized with a grievous and uncouth sickness. Some alleged it was due to poison, and others firmly declared it was smallpox. It is unlikely that we shall ever know what it was.

Mary did not hasten to see her sick husband. About the same time that he left for Glasgow, she and the Earl of Bothwell passed to Drymen where they spent five or six days in Lord Drummond's house. After that they went together to Tullibardine. The reason assigned for not visiting Darnley was that she had had a fall from a horse. As late as 20 January 1567 she wrote to Archbishop Beaton, her ambassador in Paris, referring in bitter terms to her husband. On the very day, however, when she had written to the Archbishop, Mary set out for Glasgow to see the king, arriving on 22 January. She and Darnley became apparently reconciled, and in spite of certain hints he had previously received as to possible danger, he agreed to accompany her back to Edinburgh.

Before the end of the month she had him lodged in a humble and dilapidated house at Kirk of Field near the site of the Old University Buildings, then outside the city. It was a small dwelling and George Buchanan (a contemporary) described it as 'not comely for a king'. It is a suspicious circumstance that, although Mary knew that some of her nobles were ready to assassinate Darnley, she nevertheless brought him to this abode where even the key of the door was missing. Sir Robert Melville recorded that 'many suspected that the Earl of Bothwell had some enterprise against him'.[10] So great was Mary's professed devotion now to her husband that she not only visited him by day, but on the Thursday night and Friday night before his death she slept in a room directly underneath his. On the Sunday evening she gave outstanding marks of affection. Then she suddenly left, saying she had remembered that she must be present at a masque in Holyrood House that night, and returned to the palace by torchlight. It was afterwards found

10.   D. Hay Fleming, *Mary Queen of Scots*, p. 149.

that while she was upstairs with her husband, the murderers sent by the Earl of Bothwell had placed a large quantity of gunpowder in the room she had previously occupied directly underneath. About 2 a.m. the inhabitants of Edinburgh were awakened by a terrific explosion which blew into the air the house of Kirk of Field. The body of the king was found some distance away, in the garden, unscathed by the explosion but apparently strangled.

———

Bothwell was immediately blamed, and not a few believed that the queen also was implicated. The commonalty of Scotland seemed in general to have believed in her guilt. In the vast mass of matter which has been published on this question, there is nothing more suggestive than the letter from Archbishop Beaton, Mary's faithful ambassador in Paris, telling her frankly of the reaction there. No man had ever been more loyal to Mary and his words are, therefore, all the more striking. The letter, dated 11 March 1567 warns her that nothing was so much talked of throughout Europe as herself and the present state of her realm which was interpreted in a sinister manner.

> 'He deemed it his duty to tell her that all he heard to her prejudice, that she might the better remedy it; but there was "so much evil spoken" and that so odious, that he neither could nor would rehearse it unto her. He said, however, that she was blamed as "the motive principall", and that it was even said that all had been done at her command. He earnestly urged her to do such justice as would declare her innocence to the world ... otherwise, he said, it would have been indeed better if she had "lost life and all".[11]

11.   D.Hay Fleming, *Mary Queen of Scots*, pp. 151, 152.

Mary did not take the advice of the Archbishop, nor that of Queen Elizabeth, nor that of Lennox the father of Darnley. Far from showing any suspicion of Bothwell, she showered the highest honours upon him. Within eighteen days she was at Seton with him enjoying herself in various outdoor sports. As a member of the Privy Council, he helped to make the arrangements for his own trial in the Tolbooth of Edinburgh. The whole thing was a farce and he was acquitted.

On 21 April 1567 Bothwell waylaid and carried off the queen to Dunbar. It had apparently been pre-arranged between them. It was only fourteen months since he had married the sister of the Earl of Huntly. Hamilton, the Archbishop of St Andrews who was, according to Froude, 'the most abandoned of all ecclesiastical scoundrels', now pronounced this marriage null and void, although he himself had given the Papal dispensation for it only fifteen months before. It was a disgraceful proceeding, which speaks for itself in regard to the relationship of Mary and Bothwell. Only ten days after Bothwell's divorce, and three months and five days after Darnley's murder, Mary was married to Bothwell. One month more and she was separated from him for ever.

⚬

The marriage with Bothwell filled the common people with horror and put an end to her reign. The nobles once again rose against her. Her army was defeated at Carberry Hill and she was taken prisoner. She was led into Edinburgh with her clothes torn and her hair dishevelled, amid the jeers and taunts of a multitude which hurled insults at her. The pathos of the scene has filled successive generations with a feeling of pity for the fallen queen. However much we may disapprove of her actions we cannot forget that tragedy had dogged her steps from birth. She had been dominated by forces which had wrought her ruin as a queen before attaining her twenty-fifth birthday. Her education and environment at the French court and her own impulsive and passionate nature had rendered her entirely unfit to rule the Scots in that epoch of liberation and Reformation. On 16 June 1567 she was confined in Loch Leven Castle where she signed her abdication in favour of her infant son, James VI.

John Knox was convinced of Mary's guilt, and most of the common people were determined that she should no longer reign over them. There was now no government, but the General Assembly was due to meet on 25 June 1567. It was the only channel through which the sentiments of the country could be expressed. John Knox returned from England in time to take an influential part in its proceedings. It was a gathering of vast importance for it expressed in a remarkable way the feelings of the nation, and when Parliament met on 15 December it adopted practically all the recommendations of the Assembly. It was the hour of John Knox's vindication and triumph. He must have felt that his strenuous contendings and sufferings had borne fruit at last. His good friend, the Earl of Moray, had become regent and returned from France on 22 August. The Reformer believed, no doubt, that under the rule of this good and wise Protestant the cause of the Reformation was safe. At the opening of the Parliament which met in December, John Knox preached the sermon. Since Queen Mary had never ratified the Acts passed in 1560 concerning ecclesiastical affairs, Parliament, to make assurance doubly sure, re-enacted each one of them, thus showing unequivocally its approval of the Scots Confession of Faith, the Act abolishing Papal jurisdiction and authority in Scotland, the Act against the Mass and the Act repealing all former enactments contrary to these measures. All these were duly ratified by the regent, and henceforth no-one could question their validity. The Reformation had indeed triumphed and was enshrined not only in the hearts of the people but also in the Statute Book of the Realm. There were many thankful hearts among those who loved the Kirk, but there were still many dangers looming ahead.

15

THE CAPTAINS AND THE KINGS DEPART

If there were any who thought that under the new regime the Church would have endless peace, they were doomed to disappointment. The turmoil and unrest of the time was bound to affect the ecclesiastical situation as well as the civil. What John Knox wrote to his successor shortly before he died has deep significance: 'Visit me, that we may confer together on heavenly things: for, on earth, there is no stability, except in the Kirk of Jesus Christ, ever fighting under the cross.'

On 2 May 1568 Queen Mary suddenly escaped from Loch Leven Castle. There, as elsewhere, she had fascinated the men who were around her. George Douglas, brother of the Laird of Lochleven, fell completely under her spell and made arrangements for her escape. His nephew, Willie Douglas, secured the Castle keys and then rowed the queen ashore. She made for Niddrie, then Hamilton, and soon had gathered an army of about 6,000 around her. The Regent Moray met her outside Glasgow at Langside and, although his army was much smaller, decisively defeated her, thanks largely to the ability and courage of Kirkcaldy of Grange. Mary fled from the field, and that day (13 May 1568) she covered sixty miles ere she rested. From Dundrennan she crossed the Solway on 16 May and sought refuge in England.

There, during the nineteen years of her captivity, she continued to be a centre of constant political intrigue and proved much more dangerous to Queen Elizabeth when a prisoner in her country than she had been when ruling as queen over Scotland. The Catholic powers never ceased to regard her as one of their brightest hopes. They longed to see Elizabeth deposed and Mary placed upon her throne, and there were many nobles in both Scotland and England who would gladly have lent themselves to such an enterprise. During the remainder of her lifetime, the Queen of Scots proved to be a focus of unrest, not only for her own land, but for the country which provided her with a refuge. Owing to the plots with which she was associated, Elizabeth finally signed her death warrant and Mary met her tragic end on 8 February 1587 at Fotheringay.

The years immediately following her flight from Scotland were among the saddest in Scottish history. Although the government of the Regent Moray had the support of the majority of the nation, yet there were many enemies at home and abroad. In Scotland the opposition came from three sources: first, from the supporters of the old religion; second, from the representatives and friends of the very powerful house of Hamilton who resented the proclamation of the infant Prince James as king because it shut out from succession to the throne the Duke of Chatelherault, the head of that great house; and third, from Protestants who had resented Queen Elizabeth's high handed treatment of those in Scotland whom she called 'rebels' because they resisted their sovereign, Queen Mary. These now accused the Regent Moray of being too friendly with Elizabeth. For these reasons, powerful forces were arrayed against him under the leadership of Chatelherault, Argyll,

Atholl, Seton, Herries, Maitland of Lethington and John Hamilton, the Archbishop of St Andrews. With great vigour and ability the regent quickly and completely suppressed the risings in the north and in the Hamilton territory in the west. Outwardly peace reigned; but hatred ruled in the heart of his enemies. The worst fears of Moray's friends were realized when, two years later, on 23 January 1570 he was assassinated by Hamilton of Bothwellhaugh while riding through Linlithgow. The dastardly event filled Scotland with consternation and grief. It was a sore blow to John Knox, for Moray was his son in the faith and a most staunch friend. He was, moreover, a calm and capable ruler and richly deserved the title of the 'Good Regent' which the people conferred upon him. When Knox preached his funeral sermon in St Giles' church from the text 'Blessed are the dead which die in the Lord', it is recorded that he moved 'three thousand persons to shed tears for the loss of such a good and godly governor'.

This effect of John Knox's eloquence in his old age shows, incidentally, how incorrect it is to represent the Reformer as being almost a negligible and tragic figure after 1567 as is done, for example, by Lord Eustace Percy in his otherwise interesting and arresting *Life of John Knox*. It is true that his health was much impaired after he had had a stroke in October 1570 and that from then onwards his direct participation in public affairs was much restricted; but to the end his influence remained very powerful. Thus, when he preached his last sermon at the induction of his successor in St Giles', the whole congregation, out of sympathy for the old man, followed him affectionately down to his house in the Netherbow. James Melville relates how at St Andrews a few months before, in his weakness he had to be lifted into the pulpit, yet before he was done with his sermon, he was so active and vigorous that he was 'like to ding that pulpit in blads'.[1] But even more remarkable is Melville's further statement that when the preacher entered upon the application of his text the listener became so moved that he could not hold a pen to take down notes.[2] This does not suggest that his power over men was gone.

Equally eloquent as to the esteem in which Knox was held to the end is the fact of his being visited on his deathbed by so large a number of the most important nobles in the land, eager to show their deep regard for him and their appreciation of his great services to the Church and nation.

The Earl of Lennox, who succeeded to the regency on the death of Moray, was in no way comparable with his predecessor in strength of character, political wisdom or military skill. He was chosen because he was the grandfather of the young king, but he was viewed with some suspicion because Queen Elizabeth claimed him as her subject on account of long residence in England. The Hamilton faction regarded him with even more disfavour than they had shown to the Earl of Moray, for it looked as if the Lennox family were to be next in succession to the throne and not their own chief. The same formidable forces rose against the new regent as had risen against Moray when he began his rule, and the attempt to restore Queen Mary was again renewed.

Misled by the Machiavellian tactics of Lethington, even Sir William Kirkcaldy of Grange, governor of Edinburgh Castle, now went over to the queen's party. He was brave and unselfish, and had fought with remarkable heroism and ability against Mary's army at Carberry Hill and Langside where she was

1.   Smite the pulpit into shivers.
2.   James Melville, *Autobiography and Diary*, p. 33.

defeated. His defection grieved John Knox to the end of his days for they could look back upon many years of loyal friendship and collaboration, having been together during the siege of St Andrews Castle in 1547 and having suffered together in the galleys and in French prisons for the Reformed cause.

The Civil War which now broke out was particularly ferocious and cruel. It was no longer a question of Protestant against Roman Catholic. Lethington proudly claimed that the nobles of most ancient lineage were on the queen's side. In her captivity, Mary nominated the Duke of Chatelherault as lieutenant governor of Scotland. The whole nation was divided as between 'king's men' and 'queen's men'. The dreadful feud separated the best of friends, and even children at school took sides either with or against the queen. Kirkcaldy and Lethington held the castle and largely controlled the city of Edinburgh into which large numbers of Mary's adherents flocked. Meanwhile Leith became the headquarters of the king's men.

The greatest achievement during the short rule of Lennox was the capture of Dumbarton Castle, a stronghold which had been of great value to the queen's party, for it was from there that they had communication with the French and other friends abroad. It was, at the same time, the door of entrance for foreign troops which might come to Mary's help. Its sudden capture by night was brilliantly carried out by Thomas Crauford of Jordanhill with no loss of life on his side. This event turned the balance in favour of the young king and the chances of a renewal of the French alliance were much lessened. By this time, too, Queen Elizabeth definitely acknowledged the government of King James in Scotland in a despatch different in tone from those she had previously sent. But even now she added a few words 'to keep up consistency with her championship of Queen Mary'.

In Dumbarton Castle much valuable material, which had been sent by the French in support of Mary's army, was captured. John Hamilton, the Archbishop of St Andrews, was taken with his armour on, ready to fight. He was carried to Stirling where he was charged with having been principal or accessory in (a) the murder of Darnley, (b) a conspiracy against the young king, and (c) the murder of the Earl of Moray. He was condemned and publicly hanged in the market-place of Stirling on 7 April 1571. For a long time he had been the evil genius of the house of Hamilton and the leader in most of its intrigues.

The regent's forces had considerable success in various parts of the country, but in Edinburgh neither side could claim victory. There was a constant duel between the guns of the king's men placed on the Calton Hill and the Salisbury Crags, and those of the queen's men in the castle and on the roof of St Giles', where the soldiers named the largest cannon 'John Knox'.

Although deeply grieved at heart by the defection of his old friend Kirkcaldy, Knox refrained from making public reference to him. The Reformer, however, could keep silence no longer when Kirkcaldy and his men attacked the Tolbooth prison and rescued a follower who had been incarcerated for manslaughter. From the pulpit of St Giles' he denounced in withering terms this open defiance of the constituted authority, an offence which was aggravated through being committed by one who had been a leading supporter of the good cause.

A very inaccurate version of Knox's words reached Kirkcaldy. He was indignant and demanded apologies. The Reformer was accused before the Kirk Session. The situation looked so menacing that powerful friends of Knox in the west appealed to Kirkcaldy to do no injury to the person of that man 'whom God has made the first planter, and also the chief waterer of his Kirk amongst us'. On the true version of what was said being made known, both sides were content to let the matter drop.

Those in the castle seemed bent on making as great a din as possible to wear down the nerves of the citizens. The Reformer's house at the Netherbow was shaken day and night with the reverberations of the guns for it was in the centre of the conflict. Both sides were anxious not to injure him, but he steadily refused to listen to their appeals to seek a safe place of residence. One night an enemy fired a shot through the window with intent to kill him, and if he had been seated in his usual place it is likely that he would have been fatally wounded. Even so, he refused to leave until it was represented to him that, if he remained, his friends would have to place their lives in deadly peril to defend him. He departed from Edinburgh on 5 May 1571 and passed over to Fife. One evening before he left he took his way up to the castle accompanied by his colleague in St Giles', John Craig, and John Wynram, the Superintendent of Fife. Their aim was to call on their quondam friends who now held the castle for Queen Mary. They were received by Kirkcaldy, Lethington and the Duke of Chatelherault with whom they had co-operated in former days. Since Lethington was in a frail state of body, although still mentally active, the meeting took place in his bedroom. It was a strange interview, very free and easy, but with great plainness of speech on both sides. The occupants of the castle took up the position that they represented the only lawful government in Scotland. There was the inevitable battle of wits between Knox and Lethington although both were decrepit. The latter showed himself as skilful a master as ever in the use of sophistry and rejoiced, as he had always done, to have a dialectical battle with John Knox. He had, however, the impossible task of explaining 'why he, who had become the Secretary of State under the Government of the infant king, should hold his office for Queen Mary; and why (Kirkcaldy of) Grange, who had got the command of the castle of Edinburgh, also on the king's side, should employ his command on the other.'[3] There was no loss of temper and in the end these men, who had once stood side by side in the common cause, parted in a spirit of gentle raillery, never to meet again.

The Regent Lennox summoned Parliament to assemble at Stirling on 28 August 1571. There had been no gathering of the Estates so important or so largely attended as this one since 1567. Kirkcaldy of Grange, knowing of this notable assemblage, resolved to capture all its members and destroy the king's party at one blow. Accordingly he sent out secretly from Edinburgh Castle three hundred horsemen and eighty mounted musketeers on the evening of 3 September 1571. They reached Stirling at 3 a.m. and found there was not even a sentinel to challenge them. They broke open the doors of the houses where the nobles lodged and arrested them all, the regent and the Earl of Morton among them. The latter defended his residence so valiantly that the noise roused the whole town. Instead of carrying away their prisoners with all speed, the queen's troops started looting and stealing the horses of the nobles. The Earl of Mar, governor of Stirling, meanwhile rushed down from the Castle with his men, fired upon the attackers and released all the prisoners. During this operation the Regent Lennox was treacherously shot in the back with a pistol and died soon afterwards, affectionately committing 'his poor wife Meg' to the sympathy and protection of Mar.

Once again in her tumultuous history Scotland was violently bereft of her ruler. The new regent was the Earl of Mar, a man of

---

3.   J.H. Burton, *History of Scotland*, v, pp. 57, 58.

pacific intentions who sought to establish peace in the land. He speedily found the task was beyond his strength. He discovered also that the real governor of the nation was the Earl of Morton, whose dominating personality seemed to carry all before it. In one sense this did not bode well for the Church. In the Parliament at Stirling, which had been brought to so abrupt a termination, Morton had shown a hostile attitude. The General Assembly presented a petition to Parliament, complaining that ministers were being reduced to intense poverty through not getting their rights and pointing out that 'gentlemen, courtiers, babes, and persons unable to guide themselves' were promoted by the government to benefices which required 'learned preachers'. The Assembly made the modest request that benefices be bestowed only upon persons found qualified by the kirk, and 'that incest and other grievous crimes be punished'. Richard Bannatyne relates that although 'the poor Regent Lennox approved the petitions and acknowledged them to be most reasonable', yet they were 'contemned' by this Parliament and the ministers were called 'proud knaves'. 'Morton especially, who ruled all, said he should lay their pride, and put order to them, with many other injurious words.'[4] Here we see the first manifestation of that evil policy towards the Church which was to characterize the administration of Morton. His besetting sin was avarice, and he wanted to seize for himself as much of the patrimony of the Church as possible. A great part of his wealth was obtained in that way.

It was a strange irony of fate that a peace-loving man like the Earl of Mar should have been called to rule Scotland in a year of bloody, internecine conflict. His attempts to capture Edinburgh Castle were frustrated by the military skill of Kirkcaldy of

4.   Richard Bannatyne, *Memorials*, p. 186.

Grange. In the north, Sir Adam Gordon, lieutenant for the queen in that quarter, waged a merciless war against the Forbes Clan who were king's men. In one encounter Gordon slew three hundred men and captured two hundred including the Master of Forbes. The warfare spread like conflagration throughout the country. 'Although the deeds which characterized this civil war were but insignificant skirmishes, their aggregate produced an amount of bloodshed, ferocity, and insecurity compared with which a whole campaign of national victories and defeats would have been little felt.'[5] In later days, this awful year could not be recalled without horror. Efforts to bring about peace failed until, finally, through the efforts of Queen Elizabeth, a truce for two months was signed on 30 July 1572. This truce was later extended to five months.

During the stormy events just referred to, John Knox was at St Andrews where he took up residence in July 1571 after he was persuaded to leave Edinburgh. James Melville, then a student at St Leonard's College, has left us some invaluable pen portraits of the aged Reformer at this time.

> Of all the benefits I had that year (1571), was the coming of that maist notable prophet and apostle of our nation, Mr John Knox, to St Andrews. I heard him teach there the prophecies of Daniel. I had my pen and my little book, and tuck away sic things as I could comprehend ... Mr Knox wald sumtyme comein and repose him in our court-yard and call us scholars to him and bless us, and exhort us to know God and his wark in our country, and stand by the guid caus. I saw him everie day of his doctrine (preaching) go hulie and fear[6] with a furring

---

5.   Thomas Thomson, *History of the Scottish People*, IV, p. 293.

6.   Slowly and warily.

of martriks about his neck, a staff in the ane hand, and guid godlie Richart Ballenden, his servand, halding up the other oxtar,[7] from the Abbey to the paroche kirk, and by the said Richart and another servand, lifted up to the pulpit.[8]

Melville, like some other writers, shows that in spite of Knox's physical weakness in this period of his life he had yet an amazing power of rousing himself to intense activity of mind and body when stirred up by some important question. This was the case when Morton introduced his new policy of creating bishops. By the sole direction of the Earl, John Douglas, Rector of the University, was appointed Archbishop of St Andrews in place of Hamilton. Knowing well the attitude of Knox to such questions, Morton went in person to St Andrews to make certain that the new archbishop would be duly inducted. He asked John Knox to perform the ceremony but instead of doing so, the Reformer protested with all his might against the innovation and refused point blank to have anything to do with it. While he was friendly to John Douglas personally, he 'regretted that such a burden should be placed on an old man's back', and was alarmed with the 'the high-handed action of Morton and its threatened consequences to the liberty of the Church.'[9]

Knox held that the polity of the Church had been settled already by Assemblies and Parliaments, and could not thus be changed by the will of one man.[10] Immediately before the inauguration on 10 February 1572, Knox preached before the Earl of Morton, and 'in an open audience of manie then present, denounced *anathema* to the fiver, *anathema* to the

---

7.   Armpit.

8.   James Melville, *Diary*, p. 33.

9.   P. Hume Brown, *John Knox*, II, p. 271.

10. See Richard Bannatyne, *Memorials*, pp. 256, 257.

receaver'. One cannot but admire the courage of the frail old Reformer who before the face of the most powerful and resolute man in Scotland thus denounced his pet scheme in presence of all the people. The order used in the admission of the archbishop was the same as for superintendents, and he answered the same questions.

Preaching in the Abbey two days before this, Patrick Adamson drew his famous distinction between the different kinds of bishops. There were, he said, three sorts of them: 'My lord bishop', 'my lord's bishop', and 'the Lord's bishop'. ' "My lord bishop"', said he, 'was in time of Papistrie; "my lord's bishop" is now, when my lord getteth the benefice, and the bishop serveth for a portioun out of the benefice, to make my lord's title sure: "the Lord's bishop" is the true minister of the Gospell'.[11]

John Rutherford, Provost of the Old College, maliciously insinuated that Knox's opposition to the appointment of the archbishop was due to discontent and jealousy because he himself had not been nominated. Calderwood relates that 'Mr Knox purged himself the nixt Lord's Day, in these words: "I have refused a greater bishoprick nor ever it was, which I might have had with the favour of greater men nor he hath his. I did, and doe repyne, for discharge of my conscience, that the Kirk of Scotland be not subject to that order".[12] Knox's reference was to the bishopric of Rochester which he declined when in England. His emphatic statement that he did not wish the Kirk of Scotland to be *subject to that order* is sufficient of itself to show that he objected to Diocesan Episcopacy. All this is in keeping with is pronouncements at the last General Assembly he ever attended in March 1572 when, according to

11.   David Calderwood, *History of the Kirk of Scotland*, III, p. 206.

12.   *Op. cit.*, III, p. 207.

James Melville, 'he opposed himself directly and zealously' to the making of bishops.[13] It is consistent, also, with his action in 1566 when he persuaded the General Assembly to approve the Second Helvetic Confession which clearly and definitely sustained the Presbyterian system.

In St Andrews as elsewhere, the civil war of 1571-72 caused grave dissension. The citizens were divided and so were the colleges. There were many local jealousies and much backbiting, and altogether St Andrews was not then a happy place. A member of the Hamilton faction launched a scurrilous attack on John Knox, making serious charges against him. The Reformer, however, soon brought him to his senses and compelled him to withdraw his accusations.

***

In the meanwhile, Knox's faithful congregation in Edinburgh were anxious to have him back. The times were dangerous and difficult and they needed his counsel and the inspiration of his presence. A deputation from St Giles' came to him at St Andrews urging his speedy return, and on 17 August he left for home. He was now so weak that he could not be heard in the great church and so he preached in the Tolbooth Church which was part of the same building. Knox immediately set in motion plans for calling a successor, and the choice of the congregation fell on James Lawson, Vice-Principal of Aberdeen University, whom he urged to come with all speed for he knew his days were drawing to an end.

Immediately after the Reformer's return to Edinburgh there occurred the dreadful massacre of St Bartholomew's Eve in France on 24 August 1572. This cold-blooded and calculated murder of 20,000 Protestants in one night sent a shudder

---

13.   James Melville, *Diary*, p. 31.

through all the Reformed churches. The heinousness of the crime was aggravated by the fact that a treaty of peace had been made with the Huguenots, and the king, Charles IX, did everything to persuade the Protestants that they could dwell in complete security. On this terrible night some of the greatest Frenchmen perished, men such as Admiral Coligny, the brave and wise leader of the Huguenots.

The news of the atrocious event caused intense indignation. When the French ambassador entered the court in London he found all clothed in mourning, and there was not a voice to welcome him. In Edinburgh, the terrible tidings brought John Knox such sorrow that it hastened his end, for among the illustrious dead were many who had been his intimate personal friends. He felt, however, that he had one great public duty to discharge ere he died. Before a large congregation, which included Du Croc the French ambassador, he denounced with much of his old vehemence the workers of iniquity and pointed out the extreme dangers of the situation not only in France but in other lands, for the Vatican had indicated its approval of the dastardly deed by the ringing of bells. John Knox organized a great protest movement and helped in forming a defensive Protestant league in Scotland, England and other lands. When Du Croc protested against Knox's utterances, the latter replied: 'Declare to the ambassador and bid him to tell his master that the sentence is pronounced in Scotland against that murderer, the King of France; and that God's vengeance shall never depart from him nor his house, but that his name shall remain in execration to posterity in all time coming.'

One of the immediate effects of the massacre was seriously to weaken the queen's party in Scotland and to destroy the hope of a renewal of the French alliance where that had existed. Mary had been on close and friendly terms with many

206

of those implicated in this horrible crime, and the feeling was intensified that she must never return to Scotland as queen. At the same time the distrust of the Roman Church was greatly increased and men felt it was no use signing treaties with those who believed that no faith should be kept with 'heretics'.

On 9 November 1572 John Knox preached his last sermon at the induction of his successor in St Giles', and at the close of the service he received clear evidence of how much his people loved him. They were not forgetful of his faithful ministrations during the thirteen years of storm and stress they had passed through together.

On Tuesday, 11th, he was confined to his room with a severe cough. He called his servants together and paid them their wages. Next day when he settled with one who was not present the previous day, he gave him a gratuity of twenty shillings saying, 'Thou wilt never get no more from me in this life'. In spite of his illness, the innate friendliness of his nature which was often hidden during his intense struggles in life, shone out time and again in the reception of his visitors, and even a certain sense of humour. One day, thinking it was the Lord's Day, he wanted to go to church to preach 'on the resurrection'.

Even during his illness he continued to show a patriotic interest in his country and in the events transpiring around him. His old friend Sir William Kirkcaldy of Grange seemed to be much upon his spirit. He sent James Lawson, his successor, with a message to tell him that John Knox, now going to die, was the same man that he was before when he was in full health, and entreat him to consider the state in which he was now standing, fighting for what he had so long opposed. When David Lindsay, minister of Leith, visited the dying man a day or two later, he said, 'Brother, I have desired all this day to have had you, that I may sent you yet again to yon man in the castle, whom you know I have loved so dearly. Go, I pray you, and tell him that I have sent you to him yet once more to warn him, and bid him in the name of God, to leave that evil cause and give over that castle. If not, he shall be brought down over the walls of it with shame, and hang against the sun. So God hath assured me.' Kirkcaldy was affected by the message, but when he conferred with his evil counsellor, Lethington, he sent back a coarse and contemptible answer. In the following year, forsaken by almost all, the Earl of Morton captured him after a heroic fight for a bad cause. In spite of innumerable appeals for clemency which came from admirers, the Earl insisted on his execution. When he saw the gallows awaiting him at the Mercat Cross and the bright sun shining behind it, he turned pale and said to Mr Lindsay who ministered to him, 'Faith, Mr David, I perceive well now that Mr Knox was the true servant of God, and that his threatenings are accomplished.' He was wonderfully comforted when Mr Lindsay told him that Knox believed that God would show mercy to his soul.

Another instance of the Reformer's prophetic instinct, especially in the last few days of his life, concerns the Earl of Morton himself, who refused to show mercy to Kirkcaldy. The Regent Mar had died suddenly on 29 October and it was now known that Morton was to succeed him. Five days before he took up the regency, he visited Knox and had a private interview. What transpired was not known until nearly nine years later when, after falling from power, he too was awaiting execution. He then related all the circumstances. Knox dealt with this proud man's spiritual state as if he were speaking to one of the humblest in the land. Having been assured disingenuously that Morton was not concerned with the death of David Rizzio, the dying man solemnly charged him to remember that the Lord had permitted him to have many beautiful possessions, and in God's name he called upon him to use his position and influence better in time to come 'than you have done in time past. If so you do, God shall bless and honour you, but if you do it not, God shall spoil you of these benefits and your end shall be ignominy and shame'. All this Morton himself related a few days before facing his death of 'ignominy and shame', and sorely lamented that he had not paid more earnest heed to John Knox's solemn admonitions.

Cases like those of Morton and Kirkcaldy reveal to us that the secret of Knox's power was spiritual. We are in danger of forgetting this when we see the Reformers playing their part in a tumultuous and stormy age. These two men had always respected Knox in their hearts, and in the end acknowledged that he was 'a man of God'. Here we have the secret of the great things which he was able to accomplish.

A week before he died, Knox sent for the office-bearers of his church to bid them a last 'good-night'. His words were solemn and apostolic and protested that when he had been severe it was not for hatred of the persons of men but to warn them against the vice which was in men.

Some of the greatest nobles in the land came to show their respect and have a last word with him. To each he gave a word of admonition or exhortation in spite of being in great pain.

On 23 November, a Sabbath, after lying very quiet for a time, he said, 'If anie be present, let them come, and see the work of God'. His secretary, Richard, sent to the church for John Johnston. Then Knox burst forth:

> I have been in meditation these two last nights upon the troubled Kirk of God, despised of the world, but precious in his sight; and have called to God for it, and commended it to Christ her head. I have been fighting against Satan, who is ever

ready to assault. I have fought against spirituall wickednesses, and have prevailed. I have beene in heaven,where presentlie I am , and tasted of the heavenly joyes.[14]

Here we get an insight into the spiritual life of the real John Knox.

On the evening of 24 November he said to his wife, 'Goe, read where I cast my first anchor', and she read to him the seventeenth chapter of John's Gospel. 'About halfe to tenne, they went to the ordinar prayer, which being ended, Doctor Preston said unto him, "Sir, hear yee the prayers?" He answered, "I would to God that yee and all men heard them as I heard: I praise God for that heavenlie sound". Then he exclaimed suddenly, 'Now, it is come', and as he was falling into unconsciousness his faithful secretary asked for a sign that he rested on the promises of God. 'He lifted up his one hand, and immediately thereafter rendered his spirit, about eleven hours at night.' 'After this manner departed this man of God, the light and comfort of our kirk, a pattern to ministers for holy life, soundness in doctrine, and boldness in reproving vice.'[15]

On 26 November 1572 he was buried in the cemetery immediately to the south of St Giles' Church in the presence of a vast concourse of people and all the nobility who were in town. The Regent Morton, standing by the grave, bore a notable testimony: 'Here lies one who neither flattered nor feared any flesh.'

---

14. David Calderwood, *History*, III, p. 236.

15. David Calderwood, *op. cit.*, III, p. 237.

16

CONCLUSION

It remains but to give an idea as to the state of Scotland in the year following the death of John Knox, as this is a pointer to later events.

On 1 January 1573, the five months' truce which had existed between the two parties in the civil war came to an end and immediately the guns of the castle opened fire. Under the masterly direction of the Regent Morton matters took on a new aspect for the king's party. The situation was now unfavourable for Queen Mary because of the deep impression and the terror caused by the massacre of the Huguenots in France. It was not very difficult for Morton to detach from the queen's party its leading nobles: Chatelherault and the Hamiltons, the Earl of Huntly and the Gordons, and the Earl of Argyll. Sir James Balfour observing how the wind blew as was his custom, deserted the castle. Throughout Scotland, the queen's party virtually collapsed. Edinburgh Castle alone remained as the last stronghold of this party, and from its ramparts Kirkcaldy hurled defiance at the regent and his troops. Queen Elizabeth, finding that the Queen of Scots presented her with an insoluble problem, finally resolved on the urgent entreaty of her minister Cecil, to send aid to Morton. With the help of the English troops, the regent violently bombarded some of the

strongest towers of the castle. The troops inside rebelled and
threatened to hang Kirkcaldy and Lethington if they did not
surrender. There was no alternative, so they placed themselves
in the hands of Drury the English general, an old companion
in arms of the brave Kirkcaldy. We have already noticed his fate
at the hands of Morton. Lethington died suddenly before he
could be brought to the gallows.

The Earl of Morton ruled with an iron hand. He imposed
order and peace throughout the land and, notwithstanding
his faults, this must have been an unspeakable boon after the
terrible period of war which had afflicted the Scottish people.

⚏

To understand the position of the Church in 1573 we
must think again of January 1572 and the decisions of the
Convention of Leith in that month. At the Reformation,
Parliament magnanimously allowed the archbishops and
bishops of the Roman Church to continue drawing two-thirds
of the large revenues of their sees although they were discharging
no official function. As these died out, the question arose as to
what should be done with the endowments. The nobles, led by
Morton, were determined to have them. Some show of legality
was desirable, however, and so they asked the regent to call the
Convention. There were ministers there, although they were
not appointed by any Church court and, therefore, could not
legally bind the General Assembly. The decisions were, however,
imposed by court authority, chiefly by the Earl of Morton
who was primarily responsible for this contemptible plan. It
was decided that certain ministers be appointed to the vacant
archbishoprics and bishoprics, but that they have no more power
than superintendents and be subject to the General Assembly.
The new bishops were to be little more than figureheads. It
was arranged that the patron (usually a noble, but sometimes

the Crown) should seek out a man who would accept the post for a pittance, while the patron himself drew the greater part of the revenue. The new bishops were contemptuously called 'tulchans', this being the name formerly applied in Scotland to a stuffed calf-skin laid down beside the cow in the belief that this caused her to give her milk freely. 'To draw what remained of the bishops' revenues, it was expedient that there should be bishops; but the revenues were not for them, but for the lay lords, who milked the ecclesiastical cow.'[1] In those days of civil war it was difficult for the Church to oppose Morton, for he seemed to be the only man capable of contending with the Queen Mary party. The plan therefore was submitted to with bad grace but only as an interim arrangement. As indicative of the attitude of the Church, the General Assembly which met at Perth on 6 August 1572 unanimously protested against the use of such names as archbishop, dean, archdeacon, chancellor and chapter, as names which savoured of 'popery'. The General Assembly continued to maintain its jurisdiction with supremacy over the bishops, and never retreated from the principle of presbytery, involving the equality of ministers and the authority of Church courts over all the constituent members. Nevertheless, the existence of these bishops led on to demands that they should be recognized as diocesan bishops in the fullest sense. This Episcopal point of view was strongly championed by the Stuart kings, and so arose the arduous and unrelenting struggle between Presbyterians and Prelatists which went on with varying fortunes until the last of the Stuarts was driven from the throne in 1688 and Presbyterianism was firmly established in the Revolution Settlement under William of Orange.

---

1.   J. H. Burton, *History*, V, p. 81.

In spite of these clouds on the horizon, however, the situation of the Church in 1573 gave cause for profound thankfulness. Whereas in 1560 there were not more than a dozen ministers in all Scotland professing the reformed faith, there were now over 500. In more than a thousand parishes the people were being served by ministers, readers or exhorters. Education was being rapidly improved throughout the land, and every effort was being made to raise a spiritual and a cultured ministry. Above all, the people now had the Word of God in their own language which was a boon of indescribable worth. Following its guidance men were now able to come freely to the Lord Jesus for salvation without the intervention of any human priest. The truth, moreover, was making men free, and a strong democratic nation was emerging after centuries of dictatorial oppression and spiritual darkness. In spite of all these encouragements, however, it was being found then, as it is today, that 'the price of liberty is eternal vigilance', and men like Andrew Melville, Alexander Henderson, Samuel Rutherford, Johnston of Warriston and a host of Covenanters would have to suffer with blood and tears ere the religious freedom of Scotland would be rendered really secure.

BIBLIOGRAPHY

P. Hume Brown. *History of Scotland*, 3 Vols. Cambridge University Press, n.d.

—*Life of John Knox*, 2 Vols. Adam & Charles Black, 1895.

George Buchanan. *History of Scotland*. Edward Jones, 1690.

J. Hill Burton. *History of Scotland*, Vols. IV and V. Blackwood, 1873

David Calderwood. *History of the Kirk of Scotland*, Vols. I-III. Wodrow Society, 1842.

John Cunningham. *Church History of Scotland*. 2 Vols. Edinburgh, 1859.

D. Hay Fleming, *Mary Queen of Scots*. Hodder & Stoughton, 1898.[1]

—*The Reformation in Scotland*. Hodder & Stoughton, 1910.

Taylor Innes. *John Knox*. Edinburgh: Oliphant, Anderson & Ferrier, 1896.

John Knox. *History of the Reformation in Scotland*, 2 Vols. Ed. Croft Dickinson. Nelson, 1949.

1.   Invaluable for its references to original documents.

David Laing. *Works of John Knox*. Wodrow Society, 1844.

T.M. Lindsay. *History of the Reformation*, 2 Vols. T. & T. Clark, 1906.

Thomas McCrie. *Life of John Knox*. Edinburgh: William Blackwood, 1855.

—*Sketches of Scottish Church History*. J. Johnstone, 1846.

A.R. MacEwen. *A History of the Church in Scotland*, Vol. II. Hodder & Stoughton, 1915.

Donald Maclean. *Counter-Reformation in Scotland*. James Clarke, 1931.

Donald MacMillan. *John Knox*. Melrose, 1905.

James Melville. *Autobiography*. Wodrow Society, 1842.

A.F. Mitchell. *The Scottish Reformation*. Baird Lecture, 1899.

David Patrick. *Statutes of the Scottish Church*. Edinburgh, 1907.

Eustace Percy. *John Knox*. Hodder & Stoughton, 1937.

Thomas Thomson. *History of the Scottish People*, Vols. III and IV. Blackie, 1897.

Hugh Watt. *John Knox in Controversy*. Nelson, 1950.

The First Book of Discipline.

The Scots Confession.[2]

2. See Appendices in Croft Dickinson's edition of Knox's *History*. (Nelson, 1949.)

Index

Index

Tom Lennie

"Just as Pentecost was desperately needed at the beginning of the Christian era, so another season of God-sent revival is the urgent need of this hour. A careful reading of "Glory in the Glen" will help in many ways."
Richard Owen Roberts
International Awakening Ministries

Glory in the Glen

A History of Evangelical Revivals in Scotland

1880–1940

Glory in the Glen:
A History of Evangelical Revivals in Scotland 1880–1940

TOM LENNIE

No nation on earth has a richer, more colourful, and more long-standing heritage of evangelical awakenings than Scotland – yet most people are unfamiliar with its dramatic legacy. Most historical studies stop at, or before, the Moody & Sankey Revival of 1873-74. It is commonly assumed that very few genuine revivals occurred since that date until the Lewis Revival of 1949-53. Tom Lennie thoroughly debunks this idea – showing that religious awakenings were relatively common in Scotland between these dates – and provides a comprehensive account of the many exciting revivals that have taken place throughout Scotland.

The Awakenings in the Outer Hebrides and North East fishing communities that had several unique and striking features are considered in separate sections. Revivals amongst both children/students and Pentecostals are also given separate treatment.

Of particular significance is the first comprehensive account of the 1930s 'Laymen's Revival' in Lewis. This fascinating, but near-forgotten, movement may have been even more powerful and influential than the later Lewis Revival.

Glory in the Glen tells a thoroughly absorbing, and largely untold, story. It is the result of painstaking research, conducted over more than half-a-decade, from hundreds of source materials as well as personal interviews. Much of the material has never before been published.

A native of Orkney, Tom Lennie has long held a passion for spiritual revivals worldwide, and owns one of the largest private libraries of revival literature in the UK. He currently resides in Edinburgh, where he is working on the next volume of his trilogy on Scottish revival movements.

ISBN 978-1-84550-377-2

CHRISTOPHER CATHERWOOD

FIVE LEADING REFORMERS

Lives at a watershed of history

MARTIN LUTHER
THOMAS CRANMER
JOHN CALVIN
JOHN KNOX
ULRICH ZWINGLI

"Each in his way was a watershed figure, and Catherwood's vivid profiling of them will help to keep their memory green."
J. I. Packer

Five Leading Reformers:
Lives at Watershed of History

CHRISTOPHER CATHERWOOD

Christopher Catherwood summarises the lives of Martin Luther, John Calvin, Ulrich Zwingli, Thomas Cranmer and John Knox. He unlocks the motivation, the power and the drive that pushed these men to risk their position, their livelihoods and their lives.

The Reformation upheaval of the sixteenth century had national, cultural, social and political aspects as well as opening a new era on the theological, ecclesiastical and religious fronts. Historians, like theologians, find it endlessly interesting. Here Christopher Catherwood, a writer abreast of on-going historical study of the period and aware of the spiritual issues hanging on the chain of events, tracks five major players from the cradle to the grave.

> J. I. Packer ~ Board of Governors' Professor of Theology,
> Regent College, Vancouver, Canada

His work is marked by honesty, for he does not look away from their flaws. But Catherwood also shows how their lives were touched by greatness from God, for He must be the ultimate explanation for the reformers' accomplishments. Catherwood does not merely re-tell familiar facts. He opens up their meaning and relevance, so that one is drawn into the drama with effortless fascination. As I read, I was constantly making connections with our present-day situation. It was a privilege to read this book, and it is a delight to recommend it.

> Raymond Ortlund ~ Pastor of Immanuel Church,
> Nashville, Tennessee

ISBN 978-1-84550-553-0

Christian Focus Publications

publishes books for all ages

Our mission statement –

STAYING FAITHFUL

In dependence upon God we seek to impact the world through literature faithful to His infallible Word, the Bible. Our aim is to ensure that the LORD Jesus Christ is presented as the only hope to obtain forgiveness of sin, live a useful life and look forward to heaven with Him.

REACHING OUT

Christ's last command requires us to reach out to our world with His gospel. We seek to help fulfil that by publishing books that point people towards Jesus and help them develop a Christ-like maturity. We aim to equip all levels of readers for life, work, ministry and mission.

Books in our adult range are published in three imprints.

Christian Focus contains popular works including biographies, commentaries, basic doctrine and Christian living. Our children's books are also published in this imprint.

Mentor focuses on books written at a level suitable for Bible College and seminary students, pastors, and other serious readers. The imprint includes commentaries, doctrinal studies, examination of current issues and church history.

Christian Heritage contains classic writings from the past.

Christian Focus Publications Ltd,
Geanies House, Fearn, Ross-shire,
IV20 1TW, Scotland, United Kingdom
info@christianfocus.com
www.christianfocus.com